Hardware-oriented m-D CORDIC-like Algorithms and Their Applications

Evgeny Dukhnich

Hardware-oriented m-D CORDIC-like Algorithms and Their Applications

LAP LAMBERT Academic Publishing

Publisher:
LAP LAMBERT Academic Publishing
is a trademark of
International Book Market Service Ltd., member of OmniScriptum Publishing Group
17 Meldrum Street, Beau Bassin 71504, Mauritius

ISBN: 978-3-659-52198-0

Evgueni Doukhnitch

Multidimensional Hardware-oriented CORDIC-like Algorithms and Their Applications

Abstract — *The most popular device used for a solution of plenty of DSP problems is CORDIC processor for orthogonal transformation of a plane rotation by Volder's algorithm. This algorithm have been employed in a number of special purpose processor arrays due to efficient realization of various types of linear transformations using simple hardware components.*

The dimensionality of CORDIC-algorithms is equal to two. This is the major disadvantage. A long sequence of these macro-operations is required for practical problem solving. Taking into account that very fast growth of modern VLSI technology offers a hardware realization of an ever-growing share of mathematical means it seems reasonable to speed up matrix computations by expressing them in terms of higher dimensional transformations. The present book is a short survey of research results which were published by author in this area for resent years.

TABLE OF CONTENTS

1. Introduction

The very fast growth of modern VLSI complexity offers a hardware realization of
an ever-growing share of mathematical means. It essentially raises the computer
performance. A typical application area for this kind of ASIC systems is the real-

time digital signal processing. For example, in a cellular phone, the speed of speech coding must match that of normal conversation. A typical real-time signal processing application has three special characteristics:

1. The computation cannot be initiated until the input signal samples are received. Hence, the result cannot be precomputed and stored for later use.

2. Results must be obtained before a prespecified deadline. If the deadline is violated, the quality of services will be dramatically degraded and even render the application useless.

3. The program execution often continues for an indefinite duration of time. Hence, the total number of mathematical operations needed to be performed per unit time, known as *throughput,* becomes an important performance indicator.

The majority of applications of DSP processors are embedded systems, such as a disk drive controller, modem, cellular phone, etc. Hence, power consumption is a key concern in the implementation of embedded systems.

So, special algorithms are needed to satisfy requirements of this application and VLSI-technology. Main requirements are the following:

-special fast algorithms are needed for arithmetic operations and elementary functions evaluation;

- algorithm have to guarantee needed accuracy and convergence after a fixed number of steps;

- every step of the algorithm have to consist of limited set of simple operations (addition, subtraction, shift etc.) with the same realization time;

- algorithm have to provide the possibility of decomposition into equal parts with a limited set of types;

- algorithm have to realize the highest possible typical computing procedures which are frequently found in signal processing methods.

For ensuring the previous requirements it is necessary to pick out a set of large operations (macrooperations) for programming of signal processing problems. It offers the realization of a computation process by one or several VLSI-chips.

The analysis of mathematical content of signal processing shows that the main problems are linear systems. These are the system of equations, eigenvalues, singular values decomposition, least squares, and other problems. The widespread way for solving linear algebra problems is zeroing entries in a vector or in a matrix by sequence of rotations or reflections. In many computations, it is necessary to zero some elements selectively. Givens rotations and Jacobi's method are widely used tools. The typical matrix operation for their solutions is a one-sided linear transformation of rotation for vector X with matrix P:

$$Y=PX. \tag{1}$$

The most popular device used for a solution of plenty of DSP problems is CORDIC processor for orthogonal transformation of a plane rotation by Volder's algorithm [1], [2]. This algorithm have been employed in a number of special purpose processor arrays due to efficient realization of various types of linear transformations using simple hardware components [2].

The dimensionality of CORDIC-algorithms is equal to two. This is the major disadvantage. A long sequence of these macro-operations is required for practical problem solving. It seems reasonable to speed up matrix computations by expressing them in terms of higher dimensional transformations. The present book is a short survey of research results which were published by author in this area for resent years.

The structure of this book is as follows: Section 2 describes the traditional CORDIC-algorithm and its modifications. Section 3 includes the CORDIC-like algorithms for 2-D positioning techniques. 4-D Quaternion CORDIC-algorithms are given in section4. Section 5 represents 8-D Octonion CORDIC-algorithm. Multidimensional hardware-oriented algorithms for fast Householder transform are presented in section 6. Section 7 describes Kroneker matrix product and its application for designing new hardware-oriented DSP algorithms. Section 8 shows the most important examples of applications for suggested octonion CORDIC-algorithm. In the last section, it's shown how to use CORDIC-approach to design hardware-oriented encryption algorithms with hyper-complex number systems.

2. Traditional CORDIC-algorithm

The CORDIC algorithm represents the matrix of circular rotation by angle α as a matrix product of elementary rotations:

$$\mathbf{P} = \begin{pmatrix} \cos\alpha & \sin\alpha \\ -\sin\alpha & \cos\alpha \end{pmatrix} = \frac{1}{k} \prod_{i=0}^{n} \mathbf{R}_i \tag{2}$$

where k is the coordinates lengthening factor given as:

$$k = \prod_{i=0}^{n} 1/\cos\Delta\varphi_i = \prod_{i=0}^{n} (1 + 2^{-2i})^{1/2} \tag{3}$$

and $\mathbf{R}_i$ is the elementary rotation matrix by angle $\Delta\varphi_i = arctan2^{-i}$ at the i-th iteration:

$$\mathbf{R}_i = \begin{pmatrix} 1 & \xi_i 2^{-i} \\ -\xi_i 2^{-i} & 1 \end{pmatrix} \tag{4}$$

Matrix (3) includes an operator of rotation direction $\xi_i = sign\ \varphi_i$ as a function of the angle $\varphi_{i+1} = \varphi_i - \xi_i \Delta\varphi_i$ with $\varphi_0 = \alpha$.

Transforming a vector $(x, y)^T$ with matrix $\mathbf{M}$, we have:

$$k(x', y')^T = (\prod_{i=0}^{n} \mathbf{R}_i)(x, y)^T$$

Hence the CORDIC-algorithm can be expressed as:

$$(x,y)^T_{i+1} = \begin{pmatrix} 1 & \xi_i 2^{-i} \\ -\xi_i 2^{-i} & 1 \end{pmatrix}(x,y)^T_i;$$

$$\varphi_{i+1} = \varphi_i - \xi_i \Delta\varphi_i; \quad \Delta\varphi_i = \arctan 2^{-i}; \qquad (5)$$

$$\xi_i = sign\,\varphi_i; \quad i = \overline{0,n}; \quad \varphi_0 = \alpha.$$

If initial vector is $(x,y)^T_0 = (x,y)^T$, then the result is $(x,y)^T_n \to k(x',y')^T$. So taking Y_0 = X, the result instead of (1) is $Y_n \to kPX$, if $n \to \infty$. This process is a **discrete linear transform** (DLT) [4]. It performs a sequence of elementary rotations by decreasing angles instead of single rotation (1).

The execution of (5) involves simple shift-add operations and consequently the algorithm differs by an extreme simplicity of hardware implementation at small expenditure of time.

This algorithm has two basic modes of operations - "rotation" mode (as in (5)) and "vectoring" mode as follows

$$(x,y)^T_{i+1} = \begin{pmatrix} 1 & \xi_i 2^{-i} \\ -\xi_i 2^{-i} & 1 \end{pmatrix}(x,y)^T_i;$$

$$\varphi_{i+1} = \varphi_i - \xi_i \Delta\varphi_i; \quad \xi_i = sign(y_i); \quad i = \overline{0,n};$$

$$\varphi_0 = 0; \quad \Delta\varphi_i = \arctan 2^{-i}; \qquad (6)$$

$$\varphi_n \to \arctan(y_0/x_0); \quad y_n \to 0; \quad x_n \to k\sqrt{x_0^2 + y_0^2}$$

Vectoring mode rotates the given two-dimensional vector $(x_0,y_0)^T$ up to bring it along the first canonical axis and to calculate the rotation angle in parallel. This allows to avoid of pre-computation of this angle and to process the elements of matrices in parallel at a time. The iterative character of algorithm allows organizing an iteration-level hardware pipeline. The amount of iterations n linearly depends on a required accuracy (after n iterations the absolute error is estimated as 2^{-n}).

Perhaps, single disadvantage of these algorithms is the scaling factor k, though it can be handled in many ways to reduce transformation time [2]. Besides, for a series of tasks the preservation of vector norm is not obligatory, thus multiplication by the constant can be omitted.

The modification of CORDIC-algorithm is a hyperbolic rotation with matrix [3]:

$$\mathbf{S}_h = \begin{pmatrix} \cosh\alpha & \sinh\alpha \\ \sinh\alpha & \cosh\alpha \end{pmatrix} = \frac{1}{k_h} \prod_{i=1}^{n} \mathbf{S}_i \qquad (7)$$

Using transformation with matrix S_h, the result is:

$$k_h(x',y')^T = (\prod_{i=1}^{n} \mathbf{S}_i)(x,y)^T$$

where S_i and k_h are as follows:

$$\mathbf{S}_i = \begin{pmatrix} 1 & \xi_i 2^{-i} \\ \xi_i 2^{-i} & 1 \end{pmatrix}, \quad k_h = \prod_{i=1}^{n}(1-2^{-2i})^{1/2} \qquad (8)$$

Hence the algorithm can be expressed as:

$$(x,y)_{i+1}^T = \mathbf{S}_i(x,y)_i^T \qquad (9)$$

Matrix S_i includes an operator of elementary rotation direction $\xi_i = sign\ \varphi_i$ as a function of the angle $\varphi_{i+1} = \varphi_i - \xi_i \Delta\varphi_i$ with $\varphi_0 = \alpha$. The angle of the elementary rotation is $\Delta\varphi_i = arctanh2^{-i}$, $i=1,2,3,4,4,5,...,13,13,14,...,n$. The result of transformation is $(x,y)_n^T \rightarrow k_h (x',y')^T$.

3. CORDIC-like Algorithms for 2-D Positioning Techniques

The location estimation of a mobile station (MS) can use measurement of signals with different techniques. The most commonly used techniques are: time of arrival (TOA), time difference of arrival (TDOA), and angle of arrival (AOA) [32].

The TOA technique determines the MS position based on the intersection of three circles as shown in Fig.1(a). Since the propagation time of the radio wave is directly proportional to its traversed range, multiplying the speed of light to the time obtains the range or distance from the MS to the communicating base station

(BS). Given the coordinates of BS$_j$, (j=1,2,3) as (X_j, Y_j), and the distances d_j between MS and BS$_j$, the simplest geometrical algorithm for TOA positioning calculates the coordinates of MS position (x,y) relative to BS$_1$ as:

$$\begin{bmatrix} x \\ y \end{bmatrix} = \frac{1}{2}\begin{bmatrix} X_2 & Y_2 \\ X_3 & Y_3 \end{bmatrix}^{-1}\begin{bmatrix} X_2^2 + Y_2^2 + d_1^2 - d_2^2 \\ X_3^2 + Y_3^2 + d_1^2 - d_3^2 \end{bmatrix}, \qquad (10)$$

The TDOA determines the MS position based on trilateration, as shown in Fig.1(b). Two independent TDOA measurements are made with respect to the base station that receives the MS's signal first. Once the two measurements are obtained, they are converted into range (distance) difference measurements. Such conversion is simply done by multiplying every TDOA measurement by the velocity of the signal (speed of light). Each range difference defines a hyperbola, and thus with three base stations two hyperbolas exit. The position of the base stations defines the foci of such hyperbolas. The intersection of the two hyperbolas defines the location of the MS.

There are two estimated TDOA-s $d_{j,1}$ between BS$_1$ and the j-th base station (j=2,3). Coordinates of MS position (x,y) relative to BS$_1$ can be calculated in terms of d_1:

$$\begin{bmatrix} x \\ y \end{bmatrix} = -\begin{bmatrix} X_2 & Y_2 \\ X_3 & Y_3 \end{bmatrix}^{-1} * \left\{ \begin{bmatrix} d_{2,1} \\ d_{3,1} \end{bmatrix} d_1 + \frac{1}{2}\begin{bmatrix} d_{2,1}^2 - K_2 + K_1 \\ d_{3,1}^2 - K_3 + K_1 \end{bmatrix} \right\}, \qquad (11)$$

where

$$\begin{aligned} K_1 &= X_1^2 + Y_1^2, \\ K_2 &= X_2^2 + Y_2^2, \\ K_3 &= X_3^2 + Y_3^2. \end{aligned} \qquad (12)$$

Inserting this intermediate result into the following equation with j = 1

$$d_j^2 = X_j^2 + Y_j^2 - 2X_j x - 2Y_j y + x^2 + y^2 \qquad (13)$$

gives a quadratic equation in terms of d1. Taking the positive root of it and substituting it into (11) results in the final solution.

The AOA technique determines the MS position (x,y) based on triangulation, as shown in Fig.1(c). The intersection of two directional lines of bearing with angles α_1 and α_2 defines a unique position, each formed by a radial from a BS to the MS. The simplest geometric solution with two AOA measurements α_1 and α_2 can be derived as:

$x= (Y_2-Y_1+X_1 \tan \alpha_1-X_2 \tan (\pi-\alpha_2)) / (\tan \alpha_1 - \tan (\pi-\alpha_2)),$

$y= Y_1+ (x-X_1) \tan \alpha_1$ (14)

To speed up positioning calculations, in [32] there were proposed new simple algorithms for location determination which can be implemented in hardware using, for example, a simple field programmable gate array (FPGA) chip. Only simple add, subtract, and shift operations are needed in these algorithms.

Hardware-oriented procedures. In the proposed algorithms, there are used the following three typical hardware-oriented procedures:

a) circular rotation of vector;

b) hyperbolic rotation of vector;

c) vector length incrementing.

a) Circular rotation: The circular rotation matrix M can be written as:

$$M = \begin{bmatrix} \cos\sigma & -\sin\sigma \\ \sin\sigma & \cos\sigma \end{bmatrix} \quad (15)$$

where σ is the rotation angle in radians. The *sin* function can be approximated as:

$\sin\sigma = 2^{-k}$ (16)

where $k \geq 5$ for an accuracy of $\varepsilon = 10^{-5}$, and the *cos* function as:

$$\cos\sigma = 1 - 2^{-(2k+1)} \qquad (17)$$

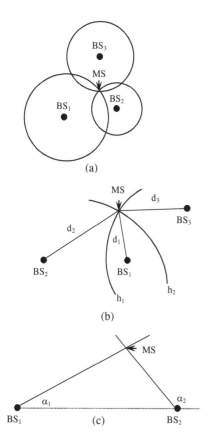

(a)

(b)

(c)

Figure 1. Position determination techniques: a) TOA; b) TDOA; c) AOA.

Therefore, as illustrated in Fig. 2, a vector (x_i, y_i) can be recursively rotated using matrix (15), and the new coordinates of its head after each rotation, are as follows:

$$x_{i+1} = x_i - x_i u - s_i y_i v \qquad (18)$$

$$y_{i+1} = y_i - y_i u + s_i x_i v \qquad (19)$$

where $s_i = \pm 1$ is a direction operator, $v = 2^{-k}$, and $u = v^2/2 = 2^{-(2k+1)}$.

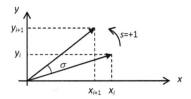

Figure 2. Circular rotation of a vector

b) Hyperbolic rotation: The hyperbolic rotation matrix M can be written as:

$$M = \begin{bmatrix} \cosh\sigma & \sinh\sigma \\ \sinh\sigma & \cosh\sigma \end{bmatrix} \qquad (20)$$

Taking the *sinh* function as:

$$\sinh\sigma = 2^{-k} \quad (21)$$

where $k \geq 5$ for an accuracy of $\varepsilon = 10^{-5}$, and the *cos* function can be approximated as :

$$\cosh\sigma = 1 + 2^{-2k-1} = 1 + 2^{-(2k+1)} \qquad (22)$$

As illustrated in Fig. 3, the parametric equations of a hyperbola are given as:

$$x = a \cosh \sigma \quad (23)$$

$$y = b \sinh \sigma \quad (24)$$

with semi-major axis a parallel to the x-axis and semi-minor axis b parallel to the y-axis.

Therefore, a vector (x_i, y_i) can be recursively rotated using matrix (20), and the new coordinates of its head after each rotation, are as follows:

$$x_{i+1} = x_i + x_i u + s_i y_i v \qquad (25)$$

$$y_{i+1} = y_i + y_i u + s_i x_i v \qquad (26)$$

where $s_i = \pm 1$ is a direction operator, $v = 2^{-k}$, and $u = v^2/2 = 2^{-(2k+1)}$, the initial values are $x_0 = a$, and $y_0 = 0$.

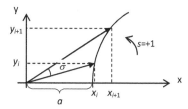

Figure 3. Hyperbolic rotation of a vector

The resultant last iterated $x_{i+1} = a \cosh\sigma$ can be used as the real x coordinate of the rotated vector. However, the resultant $y_{i+1} = a \sinh\sigma$ is not the real y coordinate of the rotated vector because of (24), where b should be used to find the real y coordinate, and thus a second stage of rotation is needed and it's as follows:

$$x'_{i+1} = x'_i + x'_i u + s_i y'_i v \qquad (27)$$

$$y'_{i+1} = y'_i + y'_i u + s_i x'_i v \qquad (28)$$

The initial values are $x'_0 = b$, and $y'_0 = 0$. Now, the resultant last iterated $y'_{i+1} = b \sinh\sigma$ can be used as the real y coordinate of the rotated vector.

c) Vector length incrementing: The first step of this procedure is to find the parameters $\sin \alpha$, $\cos \alpha$ with circular rotations using equations (18), (19) with $s_i = 1$.

The initial values for the vector are: $x_{1,0} = 1$, $y_{1,0} = 0$. Since the rotation angle in each step is σ, the accumulated angle will be:

$$\sigma_{i+1} = \sigma_i + 2^{-k} \qquad\qquad (29)$$

The stop condition for the rotation is

$$\Delta\alpha_{1i} = \alpha_1 - \sigma_i \leq \varepsilon \qquad\qquad (30)$$

and the last iterated $x_{1,i} = \cos\alpha$, and $y_{1,i} = \sin\alpha$.

A vector with polar coordinates (R, α) can be incremented in length R by increment $\Delta R = 2^{-k}$ and its orthogonal coordinates are changed as follows:

$$x_{i+1} = x_i + s\ 2^{-k}\cos\alpha \qquad\qquad (31)$$

$$y_{i+1} = y_i + s\ 2^{-k}\sin\alpha \qquad\qquad (32)$$

where s is the sign of the increment (see Fig 4). Note that a values $2^{-k}\cos\alpha$ and $2^{-k}\sin\alpha$ can be calculated once for a given constant k.

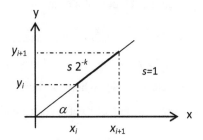

Figure 4. Vector length incrementing

So, it's clearly seen from the above equations that there is no doing any multiplications, divisions or trigonometric calculations. Instead, simple add, subtract and shift operations are used which are necessary requirement for hardware implementation.

Proposed algorithms. TOA method determines the mobile object position based on the intersection of three circles (Fig.1(a)), where each circle represents the estimated distance between the MS and the corresponding BS. The coordinates of BS$_j$, (X_j, Y_j), and the radius of the corresponding circle, d_j, $(j=1,2,3)$, are illustrated in the local coordinate system of Fig. 5. Without loss of generality, it is assumed that $(X_1,Y_1)=(0,0)$, and $(X_2,Y_2)=(X_2,0)$. The way of finding the mobile location is performed as illustrated in the flowchart of Fig. 6.

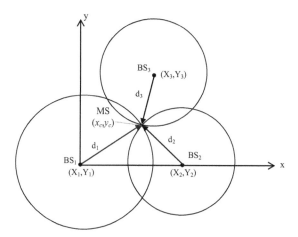

Figure 5. Local coordinate system for TOA

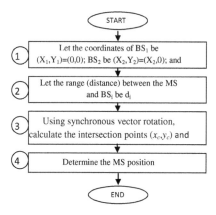

Figure 6. The TOA algorithm

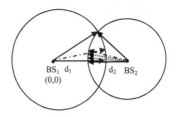

Figure 7. Idea of TOA Positioning

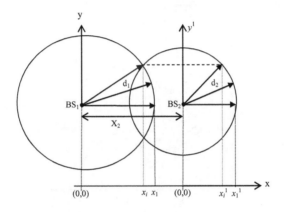

Figure 8. Synchronous rotation of

The main idea is illustrated by Fig 7. Rotation of vectors of BS_1 (d_1) and BS_2 (d_2) is needed until their heads intersect each others. An equivalent rotation is illustrated in Fig 8, where both BS-s coordinates are mapped to (0,0). Hence, the initial positions of vectors heads (x_1,y_1) and (x_1^1,y_1^1) are $(d_1,0)$ and $(d_2,0)$ respectively. Before starting vector rotations, they have to check which radius is larger. The smaller radius needs more rotations than the other one. If we assume that BS_1 has larger radius (i.e. $d_1 > d_2$), the conditions of rotation should be as follows:

While $(x_i + x_i^1 > X_2)$ & $(y_i - d_2 < \varepsilon)$

Rotate d_1

    While $(y_i > y_i^1)$

        Rotate d_2   (24)

    End while

End while

To rotate d_1 equations (18) and (19) are used with $x_0=d_1$, $y_0=0$, $s_i=1$. To rotate d_2 the same equations are used with $x_0^1 = d_2$, $y_0^1 = 0$, $s_i=1$. The intersection point (which is the estimated location of the MS) can be found as a result of these rotations. The first possible intersection point is (x_c, y_c), and the second possible intersection point is simply $(x_c, -y_c)$. Finally, the real intersection point is determined by checking the sign of the y coordinate of BS$_3$. That is, if Y_3 is positive then the nearest intersection point is (x_c, y_c), and if Y_3 is negative then this point is $(x_c, -y_c)$.

TDOA method. Referring back to Fig.1. (b), there are two given TDOA-s $d_{j,1}$ between BS$_1$ and the *j*-th base station ($j=2,3$). For linearly placed base stations, let the coordinates of BS$_1$, BS$_2$ and BS$_3$, be $(X_1,0)$, $(0,0)$ and $(X_3,0)$ respectively, as shown in Fig. 9. The parameters defining the two hyperbolas shown in the figure can be written as:

$a_1 = (d_2 - d_1)/2 = cd_{2,1}/2$ (25)

$a_2 = (d_3 - d_1)/2 = cd_{3,1}/2$ (26)

$c_1 = X_1/2$ (27)

$c_2 = (X_3 - X_1)/2$ (28)

$b_1 = \sqrt{c_1^2 - a_1^2}$ (29)

$b_2 = \sqrt{c_2^2 - a_2^2}$ (30)

where c is the signal propagation speed. The way of finding the mobile's location is illustrated in the flowchart of Fig 10.

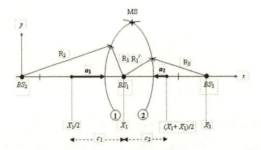

Figure 9. TDOA position determination for linearly placed base stations

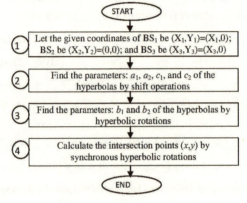

Figure 10. The general scheme for the proposed TDOA algorithm

Fig. 11 illustrates the idea of positioning the MS. Vectors a_1 and a_2 are hyperbolically rotated until their heads intersect with each other. With the coordinates being transferred to the origin points, an equivalent rotation is illustrated in Fig. 12.

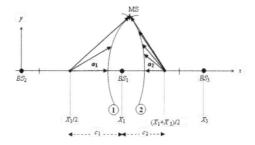

Figure 11. Idea of positioning for linearly placed base stations

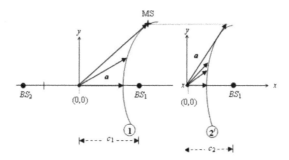

Figure 12. Synchronous rotations of vectors

Before starting synchronous rotations of the two vectors, a_1 and a_2, a check is made to determine the one with the smaller b value, since it needs more rotations. This is because of equations (15) and (18), (19) where the hyperbolic rotations of the vectors' heads depend on b_1 and b_2 in determining their next y coordinates. Hence, after rotating the two vectors synchronously one time, the vector with the smaller b value will be rotated again several times until its y coordinate equals to the y coordinate of the vector with the larger b value. Then, another synchronous rotation will be done, and so on. Hence, if b_2 is larger than b_1, then the conditions of rotation will be as follows:

While $(((c_1 + c_2) - (x_{1,i} + x_{2,i})) > \varepsilon)$

    Rotate a_2

        While $((y'_{2,i} - y'_{1,i}) > \varepsilon)$ (31)

Rotate a_1

End while

End while

To find the (x,y) coordinates of the vectors heads after each step of rotation, two stages of rotations are needed for each of the vectors. Therefore, vector a_1 is recursively rotated using (16) and (17) with initial values $x_{1,0} = a_1$, $y_{1,0} = 0$ and $s_i=1$. The resultant $x_{1,i+1}= a_1\cosh\sigma$ can be used as the real x coordinate of the rotated vector a_1. The second stage of rotation is needed according to (18) and (19) with initial values $x'_{1,0} = b_1$, and $y'_{1,0} = 0$ and $s_i=1$. The resultant $y'_{1,i+1}= b_1\sinh\sigma$ can be used as the real y coordinate of the rotated vector a_1.

To calculate b_1 in (29), again hyperbolic rotation is used. According to the CORDIC algorithm, equations (16) and (17) can be used in the rotation with initial values: $x_0 = c_1$, $y_0 = a_1$ and $s_i=-1$. The stopping criterion is when y_i becomes close to zero. The last iterated x_i is b_1. Note that more rotations are needed to approximate the value of b with larger a values.

To use the same rotation equations for the second vector a_2, the mirror of a_2 around the y axis is taken, and x_1, y_1, x'_1, y'_1, a_1, c_1 and b_1 are replaced with x_2, y_2, x'_2, y'_2, a_2, c_2 and b_2 respectively. Therefore, the new coordinates of the mirrored vector a_2 are $(x_{2,i+1}, y'_{2,i+1})$.

The intersection point $(x_c,y_c) = (x_{1,i},y'_{1,i})$ is obtained from the last iterations of rotations. The MS position (x,y) can be determined as $(x_{1,i} + X_1/2, y'_{1,i})$.

The presented idea can be extended for hexagonally placed base stations. Let coordinates of BS_1, BS_2 and BS_3, be $(X_1,0)$, $(0,0)$ and (X_3,Y_3) respectively, as shown in Fig.13. BS_3 is assumed to lie on an angle of 60^0 above the horizontal axis, where the other two base stations exist. Such angle is chosen, due to the hexagonal shape used for representing cellular networks [1].

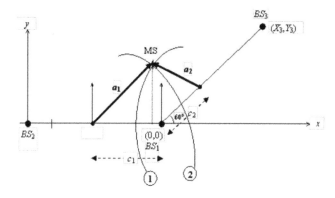

Figure 13. Idea of positioning for hexagonally placed base stations

The equations (16-19) are used to describe the rotations needed for vector a_1, and to approximate b_1, and b_2 as it shown above. However, to rotate a_2 in iteration i and get its real coordinates $(x''_{2,i}, y''_{2,i})$ on the hyperbola, it should be first rotated like for a_1 but with x_2, y_2, x'_2, y'_2, a_2, c_2 and b_2. Then, as seen in Fig.14, with local coordinates $(0,0)$ at BS_2, the point with coordinates $(c_2 - x_{2,i}, y'_{2,i})$ on the hyperbola should be circularly rotated by 60^0.

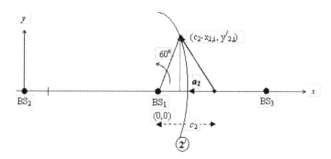

Figure 14. Idea of circular rotation by 60^0

The following equations define the rotations needed to get the real point on the second hyperbola:

$$x''_{2,i} = (c_2 - x_{2,i})\cos(60^0) - y'_{2,i}\sin(60^0) \qquad (32)$$

$$y''_{2,i} = y'_{2,i}\cos(60^0) + (c_2 - x_{2,i})\sin(60^0) \qquad (33)$$

From Fig.13, where the stopping criterion is shown, and assuming b_2 is the larger, the conditions of rotation can be written as:

While $(((c_1 - (x_{1,i} - x''_{2,i})) > \varepsilon))$

    Rotate a_2 (hyperbolic rotation followed by circular rotation by 60^0)

    While $((y''_{2,i} - y'_{1,i}) > \varepsilon)$ (34)

        Rotate a_1

    End while

End while

The intersection point can be obtained from the last iterations of rotations, and the real one can be calculated as before and written as $(x_{1,i} + X_1/2, y'_{1,i})$.

It should be noted that the multiplication by $sin(60^0)$ can be implemented in hardware using a multiple operand adder so that multiplication time is reduced to an addition time. Also, multiplication by $cos (60^0)=0.5$ can be implemented as a shift operation.

AOA system. Referring back to Fig.1.(c), we have coordinates of BS_1, and BS_2 are $(0,0)$ and $(X_2,0)$ respectively, and two AOA measurements α_1 and α_2. The way of finding the mobile's location is illustrated in the flowchart of Fig.15.

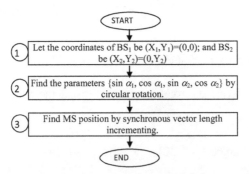

Figure 15. The general scheme for the proposed AOA algorithm

The first step of the algorithm is to find the parameters $\sin \alpha_1$, $\cos \alpha_1$, $\sin \alpha_2$, and $\cos \alpha_2$ with circular rotations of vectors using equations (9), (10) with $s_i=1$. The initial values for the first vector are: $x_{1,0} =1$, $y_{1,0} =0$, and initial values for the second vector are: $x_{2,0} =1$, $y_{2,0} =0$. Since the rotation angle in each step is σ, the accumulated angle will be:

$$\sigma_{i+1} = \sigma_i + 2^{-k} \qquad (35)$$

The stop condition for the first rotation is

$$\Delta\alpha_{1i} = \alpha_1 - \sigma_i \leq \varepsilon \qquad (36)$$

and the last iterated $x_{1,i} = \cos \alpha_1$, and $y_{1,i} = \sin \alpha_1$.

Similarly, for the second vector, the stop condition is

$$\Delta\alpha_{2i} = (\alpha_2 - \pi/2) - \sigma \leq \varepsilon \qquad (37)$$

and the last iterated $x_{2,i} = \sin \alpha_2$, and $y_{2,i} = \cos \alpha_2$.

Fig.16 illustrates the idea of positioning the MS. Vectors $\boldsymbol{R_1}$ and $\boldsymbol{R_2}$ are incremented until their heads intersect with each other. Before starting this process a check is made to determine the vector with the smaller angle value (i.e. $\min\{\alpha_1, \pi-\alpha_2\}$), since it needs more increments to achieve the same y coordinate.

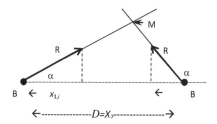

Figure 16. Synchronous vector incrementing

The synchronous incrementing can be performed with the coordinates being transferred to the origin points with mirroring as for TDOA system in Fig.12. Hence, if the value $(\pi-\alpha_2)$ is assumed to be the larger, then the conditions of incrementing will be as follows:

While $(|D - (x_{1,i} + x_{2,i})| > \varepsilon)$

      Increment R_2

        While $((y_{2,i} - y_{1,i}) > \varepsilon)$ (38)

          Increment R_1

        End while

End while

The initial values for the synchronous incrementing can be set as follows:

$x_{1,0} = \cos \alpha_1,$

$y_{1,0} = \sin \alpha_1,$

$x_{2,0} = \cos (\pi-\alpha_2),$ (39)

$y_{2,0} = \sin (\pi-\alpha_2),$

$s_i = sign(D - (x_{1,0} + x_{2,0})).$

The intersection point $(x_c, y_c) = (x_{1,i}, y_{1,i})$ is obtained from the last iteration, and it gives the position of the mobile station.

It should be noted that, if the initial values of vectors coordinates lie above the coordinates of the MS location, then $s_i = -1$, and decrementing will be applied instead of incrementing.

There is effective application the proposed algorithms for trilateration in 3-D positioning [33].

4. Quaternion CORDIC-algorithms

The mathematical tools of quaternions are used for rotation descriptions and color pixel representation. A quaternion is a hyper-complex number:

$$Q = q_0 + iq_1 + jq_2 + kq_3. \tag{50}$$

The set of such numbers has a structure of a four dimensional real vector space with a linear independent basis $\{1, i, j, k\}$. The unary quaternion with norm $N = 1$ may be represented as:

$$U = cos\varphi + (i\alpha + j\beta + k\gamma)sin\varphi. \tag{51}$$

Then the double-sided transformation

$$Y = UXU^{-1} \tag{52}$$

describes the rotation of the vector X $\{0, x_1, x_2, x_3\}$ around the axis $\{\alpha, \beta, \gamma\}$ with unit length at angle 2φ in real space. For computation (52) it is necessary to perform the multiplication of 4x4 matrices twice or to use the equivalent rule for the multiplication of quaternions. It is a difficult problem for hardware realization. On the other hand, image and orientation processing problems are described by quaternions as the most economical method. Therefore it is necessary to solve the problem of synthesized hardware-oriented algorithms for macro-operations (52).

Let us represent the transformation (52) as a sequence of elementary rotations about the angle $\Delta\varphi_1$ [4]:

$$Y = (\prod_{l=0}^{n-1} U_l) X (\prod_{l=0}^{n-1} U_l^{-1}), \tag{53}$$

where U_l is the unary quaternion of an elementary rotation. If elementary quaternions are commutative, the transformation (53) is represented as an iterative process:

$$Y_{l+1} = U_l Y_l U_l^{-1}, \quad (l = \overline{0, n-1}; \ Y_0 = X). \tag{54}$$

We have named this computing organization as the Discrete Quaternion Transform (DQT) [4]. DQT result coincides with (52) if:

$$\varphi = \sum_{l=0}^{n-1} \xi_l \Delta\varphi_1,$$

where $\xi_l = \pm 1$ is the operator of an elementary rotation direction. Let us accept for the number system with radix R:

$$\Delta\varphi_l = arctan\,(NR^{-l}),$$

where N is the modulus of the vector-axis of rotation.

Then the elementary rotation quaternion may be represented as

$$U_l = cos\Delta\varphi_l + sin\Delta\varphi_l(i\alpha + j\beta + k\gamma)/N =$$

$$= cos\Delta\varphi_l[1 + (i\alpha + j\beta + k\gamma)R^{-l}] = cos\Delta\varphi_l d_l, \tag{55}$$

where d_l is the DQT quaternion. In this case it is possible to perform the transformation (instead of (54)):

$$Y_{l+1} = d_l Y_l d_l^{-1}, \tag{56}$$

for $l=0,1,2...n-1$. As a result we will obtain the scaled vector:

$$Y_n = \prod_{l=0}^{n-1}(cos^{-2}\Delta\varphi_l)X = mX$$

The scaling factor m may be taken into account by known means without additional time used [3].

The DQT has to be supplemented with the following operations for determining the rotation direction operator:

$$\varphi_{l+1} = \varphi_l - 2\xi_l\Delta\varphi_l,$$

$$\xi_l = sign\,\varphi_l, (l = \overline{0,\ n\text{-}1};\ \varphi_0 = \varphi)$$

One iteration of algorithm (56) is easily implemented by hardware in the situation where the rotation axis parameters are chosen from the set of units, zeros, or integer degrees of the number system radix. Then all computations reduce to several addition and shift operations by analogy with the CORDIC algorithm [4]. The set of angles $\Delta\varphi_l$ are computed beforehand and stored in ROM.

Examples of algorithm designing. It is possible to get an extensive class of DQT algorithms by the changing of the rotation axis parameters. Its choice must take into account the following requirements. For the representation of the maximal rotation angle ($R=2$) it is necessary:

$$\varphi_{max} \leq \sum_{l=0}^{n-1} 2arctan(N_l\, 2^{-l}),$$

where $N_l^2 = \alpha^2 + \beta^2 + \gamma^2$ is the vector norm for the l-th iteration.

For convergence it is necessary:

$$arctan(N_l 2^{-l}) \leq \sum_{k=l+1}^{n-1} arctan(N_l\, 2^{-k})$$

Let us examine particular cases of the DQT algorithm class. If $\alpha = \beta = 0$ and $\gamma = 1$, the plane rotation algorithm appears to be a modification of the CORDIC algorithm with double steps [6]. If $\alpha = 0$ and $x_2 = x_3 = 0$, the projection of the rotated vector is determined by the ellipse equation:

$$y_{1n} = mx_1cos2\varphi,$$

$$y_{2n} = m\gamma x_1 sin2\varphi, \qquad (57)$$

$$y_{3n} = -m\beta x_1 sin2\varphi.$$

For designing other algorithms it is possible to change the rotation axis parameters (value and/or sign) from iteration to iteration depending on the coordinate signs of the vector Y_l. Let us design an algorithm for a vector modulus by determining its rotation until it coincides with the first axis. With this aim we will generate the rotation axis parameters to move the vector in the vicinity of the first coordinate axis. The rotation direction operator will be constant ($\xi_l = +1$). The axis parameter sign can be determined from Table 1. From Table 1 we have the signs of rotation axis parameters:

$sign\ \beta_l = sign\ y_{3l}$,

$sign\ \gamma_l = -sign\ y_{2l}$.

Then DQT algorithm may be expressed as:

$\xi_l = 1;\ \alpha_l = 0;$

$\beta_l = sign\ y_{3l};$

$\gamma_l = -sign\ y_{2l};$ \hfill (58)

$Y_{l+1} = d_l Y_l d_l^{-1};$

$(l = \overline{0,\ n-1};\ Y_0 = X).$

TABLE 1.

Parameter signs as functions of component signs.

Component signs of Y_l				Signs of rotation axis parameters			
Octal	y_{1l}	y_{2l}	y_{3l}	Octal	α_l	β_l	γ_l
1	+	+	+	5-6	0	+	-
2	-	+	+	5-6	0	+	-
3	-	-	+	1-2	0	+	+
4	+	-	+	1-2	0	+	+
5	+	+	-	7-8	0	-	-
6	-	+	-	7-8	0	-	-
7	-	-	-	3-4	0	-	+
8	+	-	-	3-4	0	-	+

The more general case of algorithm (58) is got when the rotated vector X occupies the same position with the coordinates $y_2 = a$; $y_3 = b$. For this it is necessary to accept $sign\ \beta_l = sign\ (y_{3l} - b)$, $\qquad sign\ \gamma_l = -sign\ (y_{2l} - a)$.

In the binary number system the single-sided transformation matrix (equivalent to (58)) can be expressed as:

$$M = \begin{pmatrix} (1 - 2^{-2l+1}) & -\gamma_l 2^{-l+1} & \beta_l 2^{-l+1} \\ \gamma_l 2^{-l+1} & 1 & \beta_l \gamma_l 2^{-2l+1} \\ \beta_l 2^{-l+1} & \beta_l \gamma_l 2^{-2l+1} & 1 \end{pmatrix} \qquad (59)$$

As a result of DQT we will get:

$$y_{1n} = m\sqrt{(x_1^2 + x_2^2 + x_3^2)}$$

$y_{2n} = y_{3n} = 0;$

where $m = \prod_{l=0}^{n-1}(1 + 2^{-2l+1}) \approx 5.3$

Presented DQT algorithms may be used for the transformation of Cartesian coordinates into polar, for the determination of vector direct cosines, vector products, etc.

Algorithm of S. F. Hsiao, J. M. Delosme. Similar to a complex number that can be written as an ordered pair of real numbers, a quaternion can also be written as an ordered pair of complex numbers p and q:

$$Q = \begin{bmatrix} p \\ q \end{bmatrix} = \begin{bmatrix} p_0 + p_1 i \\ q_0 + q_1 i \end{bmatrix} \qquad (60)$$

There is an isomorphism between the ordered pairs of complex numbers and matrix representation of quaternion in quaternion algebra [8]:

$$\mathbf{M}_Q = \begin{bmatrix} p_0 & p_1 & q_0 & q_1 \\ -p_1 & p_0 & -q_1 & q_0 \\ -q_0 & q_1 & p_0 & -p_1 \\ -q_1 & -q_0 & p_1 & p_0 \end{bmatrix}$$

To describe 4-D rotation, an unary quaternion can be taken in "polar" form (11). By following the method (2) to obtain an algorithm for 4-D elementary rotation, we can represent the 4-D rotation matrix as:

$$R_{4,i} = (1/\cos\Delta\varphi_i)M_{Q_i} = \begin{pmatrix} 1 & \alpha_i t_i & \beta_i t_i & \gamma_i t_i \\ -\alpha_i t_i & 1 & -\gamma_i t_i & \beta_i t_i \\ -\beta_i t_i & \gamma_i t_i & 1 & -\alpha_i t_i \\ -\gamma_i t_i & -\beta_i t_i & \alpha_i t_i & 1 \end{pmatrix} \tag{61}$$

The rotation parameters t_i are equal to $2^{-f(i)}$ where $\{f(i)\}$ is a non-decreasing positive integer sequence and the control signs α_i, β_i, γ_i are either 1 or -1.

Quaternion CORDIC algorithm with matrix (61) was suggested in [7] and defined by

$$Y_{i+1} = R_{4,i} Y_i , (i=\overline{0,n}; Y_0=X) \tag{62}$$

To bring real 4-D vector X along the first canonical axis, the control signs are selected according to the following expressions: $\alpha_i = f_i \cdot sign\,(y_{2,i})$; $\beta_i = f_i \cdot sign\,(y_{3,i})$; $\gamma_i = f_i \cdot sign\,(y_{4,i})$; $f_i = sign\,(y_{1,i})$. The result is equal to $kY = \left(\prod_{i=0}^n R_{4,i}\right)X$ with the scaling factor $k = \prod_{i=0}^n \sqrt{(1 + 3t_i^2)}$.

5. Octonion CORDIC-algorithms

If we have a vector X with 2 quaternion elements we can describe an 8-D rotation of equivalent 8-D real vector X. The Cayley numbers or octaves or *octonions* (8-D objects) [8] can be used:

$$Y=C*X \tag{63}$$

We can obviously consider the ordered pairs of quaternions as an octonion. Let an octonion C be represented by two quaternions p and q as

$$C = \begin{bmatrix} p \\ q \end{bmatrix} = \begin{bmatrix} p_0 + p_1 i + p_2 j + p_3 k \\ q_0 + q_1 i + q_2 j + q_3 k \end{bmatrix}$$

To represent the transformation (63) in matrix form, it is necessary to denote the linear space by its basis $\{e_0, e_1, ..., e_7\}$. Although one could make many choices for basic elements, we took the following selection [8]: $e_0=\{1,0\}^T$, $e_1=\{i,0\}^T$, $e_2=\{j,0\}^T$, $e_3=\{k,0\}^T$, $e_4=\{0,1\}^T$, $e_5=\{0,i\}^T$, $e_6=\{0,j\}^T$, $e_7=\{0,k\}^T$.

Subsequently, we can determine the matrix representation of the octonion as

$$M_c = \begin{bmatrix} p_0 & p_1 & p_2 & p_3 & q_0 & q_1 & q_2 & q_3 \\ -p_1 & p_0 & -q_0 & -q_3 & p_2 & -q_2 & q_1 & p_3 \\ -p_2 & q_0 & p_0 & -q_1 & q_2 & p_3 & -q_3 & q_2 \\ -p_3 & q_3 & q_1 & p_0 & -q_2 & -p_2 & q_0 & -p_1 \\ -q_0 & -p_2 & p_1 & q_2 & p_0 & -q_3 & -p_3 & q_1 \\ -q_1 & q_2 & -p_3 & p_2 & q_3 & p_0 & -p_1 & -q_0 \\ -q_2 & -q_1 & q_3 & -q_0 & p_3 & p_1 & p_0 & -p_2 \\ -q_3 & -p_3 & -q_2 & p_1 & -q_1 & q_0 & p_2 & p_0 \end{bmatrix}$$

This octonion has a unit norm ($N_m=1$), and can be represented in "polar" form

$$C = \cos\omega + \sin\omega(\alpha\mathbf{i} + \beta\mathbf{j} + \gamma\mathbf{k} + \delta\mathbf{l} + \lambda\mathbf{q} + \mu\mathbf{r} + \rho\mathbf{s})$$

Following (4), we can represent the 8-D rotation matrix as

$$R_{8,i}=(1/\cos\Delta\varphi_i)M_c$$

or [9]

$$R_{8,i} = \begin{bmatrix} 1 & \alpha_i t_i & \beta_i t_i & \gamma_i t_i & \delta_i t_i & \lambda_i t_i & \mu_i t_i & \rho_i t_i \\ -\alpha_i t_i & 1 & -\delta_i t_i & -\rho_i t_i & \beta_i t_i & -\mu_i t_i & \lambda_i t_i & \gamma_i t_i \\ -\beta_i t_i & \delta_i t_i & 1 & -\lambda_i t_i & -\alpha_i t_i & \gamma_i t_i & -\rho_i t_i & \mu_i t_i \\ -\gamma_i t_i & \rho_i t_i & \lambda_i t_i & 1 & -\mu_i t_i & -\beta_i t_i & \delta_i t_i & -\alpha_i t_i \\ -\delta_i t_i & -\beta_i t_i & \alpha_i t_i & \mu_i t_i & 1 & -\rho_i t_i & -\gamma_i t_i & \lambda_i t_i \\ -\lambda_i t_i & \mu_i t_i & -\gamma_i t_i & \beta_i t_i & \rho_i t_i & 1 & -\alpha_i t_i & -\delta_i t_i \\ -\mu_i t_i & -\lambda_i t_i & \rho_i t_i & -\delta_i t_i & \gamma_i t_i & \alpha_i t_i & 1 & -\beta_i t_i \\ -\rho_i t_i & -\gamma_i t_i & -\mu_i t_i & \alpha_i t_i & -\lambda_i t_i & \delta_i t_i & \beta_i t_i & 1 \end{bmatrix} \qquad (64)$$

The scaling factor is $k_i = 1/cos\Delta\varphi_i = \sqrt{(1 + 7t_i^2)}$. The rotation parameters t_i are equal to $2^{-f(i)}$ where $\{f(i)\}$ is a non-decreasing positive integer sequence, and the control signs $\alpha_i...\rho_i$ are either 1 or -1. Without performing the scaling by $1/k_i$, the implementation of one elementary rotation consists of eight concurrent shift-and-add operations. The Octonion CORDIC algorithm

$$Y_{i+1} = R_{8,i}\, Y_i\, , \, (\, i = \overline{0,n};\, Y_0 = X), \tag{65}$$

as well as original CORDIC algorithm can be used in two modes – rotation (application of transformation) and vectoring (evaluation of parameters of transformation). The usual task of vectoring in such algorithms is the annihilation of required components in a given vector, as after Volder's plane rotation, one of the two components becomes zero, while in 8-D space, seven components may be zero. A sequence of elementary rotations with matrices (64) is applied to an 8-D vector $X = [x_1, x_2, x_3, x_4, x_5, x_6, x_7, x_8]^T$ to bring it along the first canonical axis. To achieve this, the control signs are selected for (64) according to the following expressions:

$$\alpha_i = f_i \cdot sign(z_{2,i});\, \beta_i = f_i \cdot sign(z_{3,i});$$

$$\gamma_i = f_i \cdot sign(z_{4,i});\, \delta_i = f_i \cdot sign(z_{5,i}); \tag{66}$$

$$\lambda_i = f_i \cdot sign(z_{6,i});\, \mu_i = f_i \cdot sign(z_{7,i});$$

$$\rho_i = f_i \cdot sign(z_{8,i});\, f_i = sign(z_{1,i});$$

where $z_{j,i} = y_{j,i}$ $(j = 1, 2, ..., 8)$ denotes the j-th component of vector $Z_i = Y_i$, $(Y_0 = X)$, at the beginning of the $(i+1)$-th iteration. In the general case, the operands for (26) can be taken as elements of another vector Z_i. In rotation mode, the predetermined control signs are used to rotate an 8-D vector. They can be obtained from a preliminary vectoring operation, on-the-fly. The result of (65) is $kY = $

$$\left(\prod_{i=0}^{n} R_{8,i}\right)X \quad \text{with the scaling factor } k = \prod_{i=0}^{n} \sqrt{(1 + 7t_i^2)}.$$

There is no technology to prove a "general" convergence theorem for a sequence of m-D rotations, because they are not commutative and the notation of overall rotation angle does not exist. To analyze convergence, we resorted to the approach proposed by Hsiao and Delosme [16]. To prove the convergence of an m-D CORDIC algorithm over a given range, one must consider all the vectors in that range, which form a cone with the vertex in the origin in m-D space, and show that the sequence of cones that consist of all the vectors transformed after each iteration, converges toward the first axis. We observed the following successful shift sequence:

$$f(i) = \{0,1^*,2^*,3^*,4^*,5,6,7^*,8,\ldots,13^*,14,\ldots,31\};\ 1 \leq i \leq 38, \qquad (67)$$

where the sign * denotes a repetition. Thus, for 32-bits accuracy, the total number of iterations is 38 with guaranteed convergence [10].

The hardware implementation of algorithm (65) is similar to 2-D CORDIC algorithm. A possible architecture of Octonion CORDIC processor based on representation in (64) is illustrated in Figure 17. The processor is composed of shifters, which performs the multiplication using t_i, 7-to-2 Carry Save Adder (CSA) arrays, and 3 input full adders. The $S_1, S_2, \ldots, S_8$ at the top of the figure are the components where the required control signs for the next iteration are prepared, the details of which are given in (66). Owing to their ineffectiveness in the sense of execution time with respect to our design and to sustain the traceability of the figure, these components are shown separately. The products $\alpha_i \ldots \rho_i$ are used subsequently to affect the signs of the elements of 8-D vector Y_i. The I/O registers are designed such that the data transfer into and out of the processor can take place simultaneously. In Figure 17, components labeled as -1 are used to change a sign of operand.

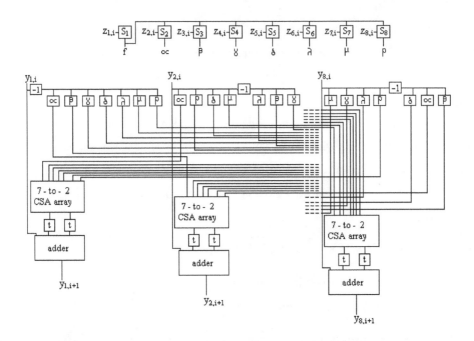

Fig. 17. Octonion CORDIC-processor architecture

6. Fast Householder Transform

The widespread way for solving linear algebra problems is zeroing entries in a vector or a matrix. Householder reflections are exceedingly useful for introducing zeros on a grand scale, e.g. the annihilation of all but the first component of a vector. The Householder transform (reflection)

$$A'=PA \qquad (68)$$

is intended for triangularization of matrix A and has a matrix [11]:

$$P = I - ww^T, \qquad (69)$$

where w – real vector $(w^Tw = 2)$, I – unit matrix. For DLT algorithm we can take a matrix product and represent the process (68) as a sequence of elemental reflections

$$P = \prod_{i=0}^{n} P_i \qquad (70)$$

with vector $w_i^T = (-2^{-i}c_1^{(i)}, c_2^{(i)})$ for $m=2$, where $c_1^{(i)}$ and $c_2^{(i)}$ – direction operators (+1 or –1) for every coordinate. In this case $w_i^T w_i = k_i \neq 2$. Therefore, the matrix of elemental reflection is modified by

$$P_i = k_i^{-1}(k_i I - 2w_i w_i^T) = k_i^{-1} T_i, \qquad (71)$$

where

$$T_i = \begin{bmatrix} 1 - 2^{-2i} & -2^{-i+1}c_1^{(i)}c_2^{(i)} \\ -2^{-i+1}c_1^{(i)}c_2^{(i)} & 2^{-2i} - 1 \end{bmatrix}$$

So the fast Householder algorithm (FHT) for $m=2$ is

$$\left. \begin{aligned} A_{i+1} &= T_i A_i, \\ c_1^{(i)} &= \text{sign } a_{11}^{(i)}, \\ c_2^{(i)} &= \text{sign } a_{21}^{(i)}, \end{aligned} \right\} \qquad (72)$$

$$i = 0, 1, ..., n; \ A_0 = A,$$

$$A_n \to kPA, \text{ if } n \to \infty.$$

This algorithm looks very much like the CORDIC-algorithm in vector-mode because the reflection is a non-proper rotation. In Figure 18 three transform steps are shown when initial vector is falling towards the axis Oa_{11}.

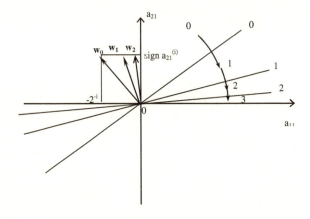

Fig. 18. The elementary reflections for $i = 0, 1, 2$.

The first column of matrix A will take the form: $a_{11}^{(n)} \approx (a_{11}^2 + a_{21}^2)$, $a_{21}^{(n)} \approx 0$.

The multiplication by the matrix T_i is reduced to some simple operations (additions and shifts). The elements of matrix (31) are constants. It is only necessary to determine to determine their signs. The main disadvantage of algorithm (8) is the scaling effect with coefficient $k = \prod_i k_i = \prod_i (1 + 2^{-2i})$. This disadvantage may be corrected by known methods for CORDIC-algorithms [2, 12].

The FHT-algorithm may be extended for an m-dimensions case. For the first column transformation of matrix A the reflection vector will take the form of:

$$w_i = (-2^{-i}c_1^{(i)}, c_2^{(i)}, ..., c_m^{(i)}), \tag{73}$$

where $c_j^{(i)} = sign\ a_{j1}^{(i)}$ $(j = 1, 2, ..., m;\ i = 0, 1, 2, ..., n)$.

Transformation (72) may be written in "column" form [13] for m-dimensions:
$$a_j^{(i+1)} = a_j^{(i)} - \alpha_j^{(i)} w_i,$$
$$\alpha_j^{(i)} = 2(m - 1 + 2^{-i})^{-1} w_i^T a_j^{(i)}, \tag{74}$$
$$j = 1, 2, ..., m,$$
$$i = 0, 1, 2, ..., n;\ a_j^{(0)} = a_j.$$

The result of (74) will be matrix (68). There is the scaling effect with the coefficient $k = \prod_{i=0}^{n} 2(m - 1 + 2^{-i})$.

FHT convergence. The area of FHT convergency is the same as CORDIC-algorithm (for $m=2$). However it reduces for $m>2$. It takes place because the directing angles (between vector w_i and axis Oa_{11}) are reduced with the increase of m: $\beta^{(i)} = arctan\ 2^{-i}/(m-1)^{1/2} \to 0$ and their sum doesn't overlap the range $[-\pi/2, +\pi/2]$.

There are two ways for keeping this range: slowing down the reduction of value $\beta^{(i)}$ or the introduction of new members in a series of $\beta^{(i)}$. The value of n must be increased in both cases, as a repetition of some first steps, for example. It is determined by experiment for particular values of m.

It is possible to reduce value of n in half if the difference between vector w_i and vector w from (2) is reduced. For FHT realization with floating-point data it is possible to determine the vector w_j using the element exponents:

$$c_j^{(i)} = sign\ a_{j1}^{(i)}\ ord\ (a_{j1}^{(i)}),\ (j = 1, 2, ..., m)$$

The complexity of the algorithm increases slightly.

Computational structures for FHT. The hardware realization of FHT is like the CORDIC-processor. It may be sequential or pipeline processing. The set of m units $u_j^{(i)}$ is required for the computation matrix (70) for step i. Units connection is shown in Figure 19. Every unit performs algorithm (74). The macropipeline with $(m-1)$ such sets may be utilized for the computation of an overtriangular matrix. Units number for j-th set (stage of macropipeline) is less by $(j-1)$ units.

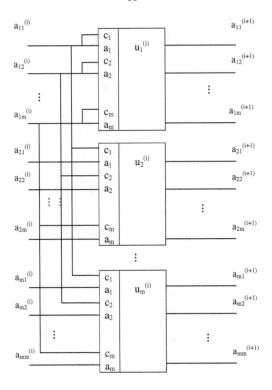

Fig.19. Units connection for *i*-th iteration of matrix (74) computation.

Householder CORDIC algorithm of J.M. Delosme and S.F. Hsiao. For *m* dimensions, Householder reflections are exceedingly useful for introducing zeros on a grand scale e.g. the annihilation of all except the first *(r-1)* components of a column A_j of matrix *A* to force $a_{r,j}$ *(r=j+1,...,m; j=1,2,...,m)* to zero for the left-side sequence of reflections in (70). J.M. Delosme and S.F. Hsiao presented the Householder CORDIC algorithm (HCA) [7] for which elementary reflection matrix U_i is:

$$U_i=(1/(1+(m-1)t_i^2))(\ 1 \oplus S_i)\times \tag{75}$$

$$\times \begin{pmatrix} 1-(m-1)t_i^2 & 2t_i & 2t_i & \dots & 2t_i \\ -2t_i & 1+(m-3)t_i^2 & -2t_i^2 & \dots & -2t_i^2 \\ -2t_i & -2t_i^2 & 1+(m-3)t_i^2 & \dots & -2t_i^2 \\ \dots & \dots & \dots & \dots & \\ -2t_i & -2t_i^2 & -2t_i^2 & \dots & 1+(m-3)t_i^2 \end{pmatrix} (1 \oplus S_i),$$

where the parameters t_i are equal to $2^{-f(i)}$ with $\{f(i)\}$ a non-decreasing positive integer sequence. The control signs in the i-th CORDIC iteration have been gathered in the direct sum:

$$1 \oplus S_i = \begin{pmatrix} 1 | & 0 & 0 & \dots & 0 \\ -- & -- & -- & -- & -- \\ 0 | & \delta_{2,i} & 0 & \dots & 0 \\ 0 | & 0 & \delta_{3,i} & \dots & 0 \\ . | & . & 0 & . & \\ . | & . & . & . & . \\ . | & . & . & & . \\ 0 | & 0 & 0 & \dots & \delta_{m,i} \end{pmatrix},$$

where the control signs are either 1 or -1:

$$\delta_{j,i} = f_i\ sign\ (a_{r,j}),\ f_i = sign(a_{r-1,i})\ (r=j+1,...,m;\ j=1,2,...,m) \tag{76}$$

for column A_j. To simplify a hardware realization they use matrix

$R_i = (1+(m-1)t_i^2)U_i.$

7. Kroneker Matrix Product and Its Application for Synthesis of Hardware-oriented DSP Algorithms

Kronecker product of matrices and its properties There are many DSP-algorithms containing sine-cosine products calculations like 2-D projections, coordinate system transformations in navigation, multi-angle rotations in kinematics, two-sided rotations (Jacobi's method), etc. Most of these algorithms can be implemented using a sequence of one-sided orthogonal transformations of a plane rotation by Volder's algorithm. The paper deals with new fast implementation of these rotations using a substitution of similarity transformation with Kronecker product of CORDIC-matrices. This substitution allows decreasing costs in time and hardware.

If A is an $N \times G$ matrix and B is a $F \times L$ matrix, then the Kronecker product is the $NF \times GL$ block matrix. For example, if N=G=F=L=2, then the Kronecker (direct) product (KP) of 2×2 matrices A and B is as follows:

$$P = \mathbf{A} \otimes \mathbf{B} = \begin{pmatrix} a_{11}\mathbf{B} & a_{12}\mathbf{B} \\ a_{21}\mathbf{B} & a_{22}\mathbf{B} \end{pmatrix} = \begin{pmatrix} a_{11}b_{11} & a_{11}b_{12} & a_{12}b_{11} & a_{12}b_{12} \\ a_{11}b_{21} & a_{11}b_{22} & a_{12}b_{21} & a_{12}b_{22} \\ a_{21}b_{11} & a_{21}b_{12} & a_{22}b_{11} & a_{22}b_{12} \\ a_{21}b_{21} & a_{21}b_{22} & a_{22}b_{21} & a_{22}b_{22} \end{pmatrix}. \quad (77)$$

For designing hardware-oriented algorithms the following properties of this operation are of most importance:

1) For arbitrary matrices A, B, C and D the following is fulfilled:

$(A \otimes B)(C \otimes D) = (AC) \otimes (BD)$.

2) If A and B are 2×2 matrices and elements of matrix $\mathbf{X} = \begin{pmatrix} x_{11} & x_{12} \\ x_{21} & x_{22} \end{pmatrix}$ are put into a form

of a 4-D vector $\mathbf{x} = (x_{11},\ x_{12},\ x_{21},\ x_{22})^T$, then the result components of the following transformations are identical also:

$\mathbf{Y} = \mathbf{A}\mathbf{X}\mathbf{B}^T \Leftrightarrow \mathbf{y} = (\mathbf{B} \otimes \mathbf{A})\mathbf{x}$. \hfill (78)

In general for arbitrary matrices, the product of a Kronecker product times a vector is as follows:

$$(\mathbf{B} \otimes \mathbf{A})\mathbf{x} = vec(\mathbf{A}\mathbf{X}\mathbf{B}^T)$$

with $\mathbf{x} = vec(\mathbf{X}^T)$ [14]. Here, the operator $vec(\mathbf{X})$ creates a vector by stringing together, one-by-one, the columns of matrix $\mathbf{X}$.

The multiplicands of KP may be matrices of plane rotation. For example, if we use two rotation matrices (2) then the KP product can be shown as:

$$\mathbf{M}_1 \otimes \mathbf{M}_2 = \begin{pmatrix} c_1 c_2 & c_1 s_2 & s_1 c_2 & s_1 s_2 \\ -c_1 s_2 & c_1 c_2 & -s_1 s_2 & s_1 c_2 \\ -s_1 c_2 & -s_1 s_2 & c_1 c_2 & c_1 s_2 \\ s_1 s_2 & -s_1 c_2 & -c_1 s_2 & c_1 c_2 \end{pmatrix} \qquad (79)$$

where $c_j = cos\alpha_j$ and $s_j = sin\alpha_j$ (j=1,2). Thus, we can calculate at once (as integrated macro operation) any sine-cosine products or their sum using this KP if we apply Volder's technique on them. The corresponding transformation can be written as

$$\mathbf{y} = (\mathbf{M}_1 \otimes \mathbf{M}_2)\mathbf{x} \qquad (80)$$

This describes a rotation by angle α_1 of a 4-D vector $\mathbf{x} = (a, b)^T$, whose 2-D components $a = (x_{11}, x_{12})^T$ and $b = (x_{21}, x_{22})^T$ are rotated by angle α_2 simultaneously. It is the same as a two-sided rotation transformation

$$Y = M_2 X M_1^T \qquad (81)$$

for 2×2 matrix X with the same components as for vector $\mathbf{x}$ in view of property 2. In contrast to multi-dimensional rotations, we implement "multi-angular" rotations or a transformation of components of a second-rank covariant tensor.

Substituting each rotation with a sequence of rotations by angles $\xi_{1i}\Delta\varphi_i$ and $\xi_{2i}\Delta\varphi_i$, in view of the property 1, we obtain [15]:

$$k^2 \mathbf{y} = \left(\left(\prod_{i=0}^{n} R_i(\xi_{2i}) \right) \otimes \left(\prod_{i=0}^{n} R_i(\xi_{1i}) \right) \right) \mathbf{x} = \left(\prod_{i=0}^{n} (R_i(\xi_{2i}) \otimes R_i(\xi_{1i})) \right) \mathbf{x} \qquad (82)$$

Spreading the offered technique (as a theoretical generalization), we have deduced algorithm for a hardware implementation of linear transformation with rotations of a 2^m-

dimensional (in view of property 2) vector simultaneously by m angles. This tensor transformation has 2^m- dimensional square matrix $P = P_m \otimes (P_{m-1} \otimes \ldots (P_2 \otimes P_1) \ldots)$ with elements equal to sine-cosine products of m angles, and can be represented as

$$k^m \mathbf{y} = \left(\prod_{i=1}^{n} (\mathbf{R}_{mi} \otimes (\mathbf{R}_{(m-1)2i} \otimes \ldots (\mathbf{R}_{2i} \otimes \mathbf{R}_{1i}) \ldots) \right) \mathbf{x} == \left(\prod_{i=0}^{n} \overset{m}{\underset{j=1}{K}} \mathbf{R}_{ji} \right) \mathbf{x}, \qquad (83)$$

where $\mathbf{K}$ denotes Kronecker matrices product . In this case required iterative algorithm looks like:

$$\left. \begin{array}{l} \mathbf{y}_{i+1} = \left(\overset{m}{\underset{j=1}{K}} \mathbf{R}_{ji} \right) \mathbf{y}_i; \quad \varphi_{j(i+1)} = \varphi_{ji} - \xi_{ji} \Delta \varphi_i; \\[3mm] \xi_{ji} = sign \varphi_{ji}; \quad j = \overline{1,m}; \quad i = \overline{0,n}; \quad \varphi_{j0} = \alpha_j; \quad \mathbf{y}_0 = \mathbf{x} \end{array} \right\} . \qquad (84)$$

It is clear that algorithm (5) is a special case of (44) with $m = 1$. For practice, the most important case is with $m = 2$ because the transformation (81) is exactly the Jacobi 2×2 SVD. Iterative algorithm for a hardware implementation of equivalent transformation (82) will be noted as

$$\left. \begin{array}{l} \begin{pmatrix} y_1 \\ y_2 \\ y_3 \\ y_4 \end{pmatrix}_{i+1} = \begin{pmatrix} 1 & \gamma_{2i} & \gamma_{1i} & \gamma_{1i}\gamma_{2i} \\ -\gamma_{2i} & 1 & -\gamma_{1i}\gamma_{2i} & \gamma_{1i} \\ -\gamma_{1i} & -\gamma_{1i}\gamma_{2i} & 1 & \gamma_{2i} \\ \gamma_{1i}\gamma_{2i} & -\gamma_{1i} & -\gamma_{2i} & 1 \end{pmatrix} \begin{pmatrix} y_1 \\ y_2 \\ y_3 \\ y_4 \end{pmatrix}_i \\[10mm] \gamma_{ji} = \xi_{ji} 2^{-i}; \varphi_{j(i+1)} = \varphi_{ji} - \xi_{ji} \Delta \varphi_i; \xi_{ji} = sign \ (\varphi_{ji}); \\[2mm] j = \overline{1,2}; i = \overline{0,n}; \ \varphi_{j0} = \alpha_j; \ \mathbf{y}_0 = \mathbf{x} = vec(\mathbf{X}), \\[2mm] \mathbf{y}_n \to vec(\mathbf{Y}) \end{array} \right\} \qquad (85)$$

The KP algorithms (85), as well as CORDIC algorithm, can be used in two modes - rotation (application of transformation) and vectoring (evaluation of a parameter of transformation). The algorithm (85) is an example of the rotation mode. Usual task of vectoring in such algorithms is annihilation of required components in a vector (matrix) given. As after plane Volder's rotation one of two components is zero, in multi-angular algorithms more than one component may be zero. A modification of the algorithm (85) for vectoring mode with

$$\xi_1 = sign \ (y_{2i}), \quad \xi_2 = sign \ (y_{3i}) \qquad (86)$$

can zero 2 of 4 components x_2 and x_3 for vector $\mathbf{x}$ corresponding to symmetric matrix X. Choice of rotation directions by the following rule:

$$\xi_1 = \xi_2 = sign\,(y_{2i} + y_{3i}) \qquad\qquad (87)$$

ensures transformation of an arbitrary 4×1 vector to vector with $x_2 = -x_3$. Accordingly, the use of a KP algorithm in vectoring mode first with signs (87) and then - (86) will ensure annihilation of the second and third component of any given vector to get the diagonal 2×2 matrix as Jacobi's method.

Convergence of KP algorithm. Considering two-sided transformation with matrix (2) for *i*-th iteration of algorithm (81) ignoring scaling factor it is possible to note that there are 4 combinations of ξ_1 and ξ_2. As for 2 cases $\xi_1 = -\xi_2$, we have

$$y_{1(i+1)} - y_{4(i+1)} = y_{1i} - y_{4i},$$

$$y_{2(i+1)} + y_{3(i+1)} = y_{2i} + y_{3i}.$$

In case $\xi_1 = \xi_2 = 1$ we have

$$y_{1(i+1)} - y_{4(i+1)} = (y_{1i} - y_{4i})cos2\,\Delta\varphi_i + (y_{2i} + y_{3i})sin2\,\Delta\varphi_i,$$

$$y_{2(i+1)} + y_{3(i+1)} = -(y_{1i} - y_{4i})sin2\,\Delta\varphi_i + (y_{2i} + y_{3i})cos2\,\Delta\varphi_i.$$

In case $\xi_1 = \xi_2 = -1$ we have

$$y_{1(i+1)} - y_{4(i+1)} = (y_{1i} - y_{4i})cos2\,\Delta\varphi_i - (y_{2i} + y_{3i})sin2\,\Delta\varphi_i,$$

$$y_{2(i+1)} + y_{3(i+1)} = (y_{1i} - y_{4i})sin2\,\Delta\varphi_i + (y_{2i} + y_{3i})cos2\,\Delta\varphi_i.$$

In other words, the rotation of a vector $(y_1 - y_4,\ y_2 + y_3)^T$ is executed by angle $2\Delta\varphi_i$. This process is known as "double CORDIC iterations" [6]. To guarantee the convergence of this algorithm according to [19] two conditions must be met:

$$\pi \le \sum_{i=0}^{n} 2\Delta\varphi_i \quad and \quad \Delta\varphi_s \le \sum_{i=s+1}^{n}\Delta\varphi_i, \quad s = \overline{0, n-1}.$$

and it's shown that both conditions are met and therefore the algorithm converges. In vectoring mode the algorithm (85) together with (87) should zero the sum $(y_{2n} + y_{3n})$. Thus, the deviation of a vector from the needed position will be no more than $2\Delta\varphi_n = 2arctan2^{-n}$.

So, in view of KP property 1 convergence of KP algorithm (85) is implied by the convergence of CORDIC-algorithm. Thus, in rotation mode the transformation simultaneously by two angles in algorithm (85) requires the same amount of iterations as CORDIC-algorithm.

Quantization Effects of the KP Algorithms: Following [17] we can analyze two types of quantization error: an approximation error due to the quantized representation of rotation angle and a rounding error due to the finite precision representation in fixed point arithmetic.

Rotation angles α_1 and α_2 in (81) are represented with approximation error δ which is bounded by the smallest rotation angle σ. That is

$$|\delta_1| = |\delta_2| = |\delta| \le \sigma = \arctan 2^{-n} \tag{88}$$

If $V_0(n)$ is the ideal result vector (85) of total rotation when $\delta = 0$, it can be computed as:

$$V_0(n) = DV(n) = \begin{pmatrix} \cos\delta_1 & -\sin\delta_1 \\ \sin\delta_1 & \cos\delta_1 \end{pmatrix} \otimes \begin{pmatrix} \cos\delta_2 & -\sin\delta_2 \\ \sin\delta_2 & \cos\delta_2 \end{pmatrix} V(n) , \tag{89}$$

where $V(n) = [y_{1n}, y_{2n}, y_{3n}, y_{4n}]^T$ is a vector with the final coordinates. Using I as 4×4 identity matrix we have

$$V_0(n) - V(n) = (D - I)V(n) \tag{90}$$

Hence, the *relative approximation error* is bounded by [17]

$$|V_0(n) - V(n)| / V(n) \le \|D - I\| \tag{91}$$

The spectral norm of matrix difference in (91) can be estimated as:

$$\|D - I\| = \sqrt{2 - 2\cos\delta_1 \cos\delta_2} = \sqrt{2}\sin|\delta| \le \sqrt{2}|\delta| \le \sqrt{2}\sigma = \sqrt{2}\arctan 2^{-n} \tag{92}$$

To guarantee an error not greater than for CORDIC algorithm we can add one extra rotation with angle $\Delta\varphi_{n+1} = \arctan 2^{n-1}$. In this case (comparing with [17]) we have:

$$\|D-I\| \le \sqrt{2}\arctan 2^{-n-1} < 2|\sin(\delta/2)| \tag{93}$$

The *rounding error* can be described with a quantization operator $Q[V(j)]$ [17] such that $Q[V(j)] = V(j) + e(j)$, where $e(j) = [e_{y1}(j), e_{y2}(j), e_{y3}(j), e_{y4}(j)]^T$ is an error due to rounding. For fixed point arithmetic, the absolute rounding error will be bounded by

$$|e_{y1}(j)| \le \varepsilon, \quad |e_{y2}(j)| \le \varepsilon, \quad |e_{y3}(j)| \le \varepsilon, \quad \text{and} \quad |e_{y4}(j)| \le \varepsilon,$$

where the magnitude of "ε" depends on the machine accuracy (for h bits accuracy $\varepsilon = 2^{-h-1}$). Hence, an upper bound for $|e(j)|$ is

$$|e(j)| = \sqrt{e_{y1}^2(j) + e_{y2}^2(j) + e_{y3}^2(j) + e_{y4}^2(j)} \le 2\varepsilon \tag{94}$$

Taking into account two error components (the rounding error propagated from the previous rotation step and the new rounding error introduced in the present step) we can use the overall rounding error propagation formula from [17] as

$$f(n) = Q[V(n)] - V(n) = e(n) + \sum_{j=0}^{n-1}\{M(j)e(j)\}, \tag{95}$$

where $M(j) = R_j(\xi_{1j}) \otimes R_j(\xi_{2j})$ is taken from (92).

So, the worst case rounding error is equal to:

$$|f(n)| \le 2\varepsilon\left(1 + \sum_{j=0}^{n-1}\|M(j)\|\right),$$

where $\|M(j)\| = \prod_{i=j}^{n} k_i^2 = \prod_{i=j}^{n}(1 + 2^{-2i})$.

Hence the overall quantization error becomes

$$E = |V(n) - V_0(n)| \le \|D^{-1} - I\|\|V_0(n)\| + |f(n)|, \tag{96}$$

where $\|D^{-1} - I\| = \|D - I\|$.

Simulation results. In our analysis Matlab 7.0 package was used. We wrote programs to implement a Jacobi method as two-side rotation for 2×2 real matrix X and to implement KP-algorithm (85) for 4-D vector x with the same components. Following [17], the experiments were repeated for many arbitrary (random) input components and random pairs of angles α_1 and α_2 to guarantee the 95% confidence level. Each random number is drawn from a uniform distribution over the interval [0,1]. Fig.20 shows the related simulation results. In the figure, the resultant number of effective binary digits was found versus the number of iterations for three values of registers length (8, 16, and 32 bits). The number of effective digits was calculated for simulated worst case error bound E as $d_{eff} = -\log_2 E - 1$.

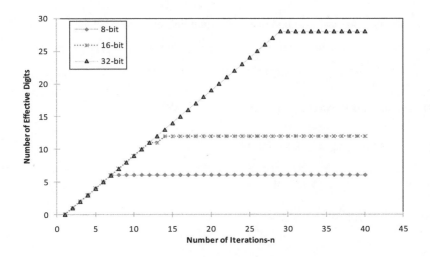

Fig. 20. Number of effective digits

The predicted worst case error bound (96) was used to plot the difference between the theoretically predicted numbers of effective digits and simulated one (see Fig.21). The figure shows that maximum difference is around 2.5 bits.

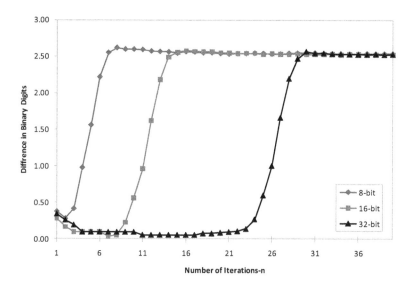

Fig.21. Difference between predicted and simulated number of effective digits

Processor architecture. The hardware implementation of algorithm (85) is similarly to base CORDIC-processor. The major components are shifters that perform right-shift by i and $2i$ bit positions, 4 carry-save-adders that transform 4 operands into 2, 4 adders, and 4 storage registers. The processor architecture is illustrated in Fig.22. It is cheaper than the simplest CORDIC implementation of two-sided rotation which requires 2 CORDIC-processors and 10 adders [16]. The proposed processor can calculate a two-sided rotation in roughly the same time as standard 2-D CORDIC-processor calculates one-side rotation because the latency distinction is one carry-save-addition only.

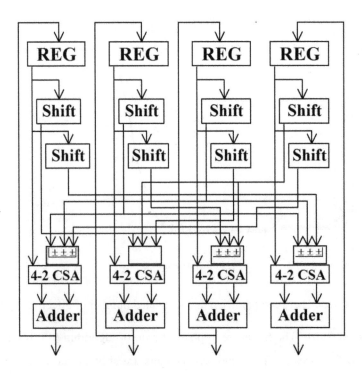

Figure 22. Processor architecture

Key applications of KP algorithms. The suggested approach can be used for several applications. Bellow are some to be mentioned.

1. *Vector projection*: A particular case of algorithm (45) is when $\varphi_{10}=\varphi_{20}=\Theta$. Taking x $=\{a, b, 0, 0\}^T$ we can implement a 2-D projection of a vector $(a, b)^T$ onto the "Θ-direction" in x-y plan with projection matrix P as

$$P = \begin{pmatrix} \cos^2\Theta & \sin\Theta\cos\Theta \\ \sin\Theta\cos\Theta & \sin^2\Theta \end{pmatrix} \qquad (97)$$

As a result of (45) we have $y_{1n} = k^2 X_p$, $y_{3n} = -k^2 Y_p$, where X_p, Y_p are coordinates of the transformed vector.

2. *Coordinate system transformation:* For example, to transform spherical coordinates (R, Θ, φ) to Cartesian (X, Y, Z), where $X = R \cos \Theta \sin \varphi$, $Y = R \sin \Theta \sin \varphi$, and $Z =$

$R\ cos\ \varphi$, we can use algorithm (85) with $x = \{0,\ 0,\ 0,\ R\}^T$ and $\alpha_1 = \Theta$, $\alpha_2 = \varphi$, and algorithm (5) with $x = \{R,\ 0\}^T$ and $\alpha = \varphi$ in parallel. As a result of (85), we have $y_{3n} = k^2\ X$, $y_{1n} = k^2\ Y$, and for (5) we have $y_{1n} = k\ Z$. Similar idea can be used to transform coordinates $(a,\ c,\ v,\ \upsilon)$ of a navigation position on a hyperboloid of revolution to Cartesian $(X,\ Y,\ Z)$ where $X = a\ cosh\ v\ cos\ \upsilon$, $Y = a\ cosh\ v\ sin\ \upsilon$, and $Z = c\ sinh\ v$. For this, KP of matrix (2) and matrix (7) with vector $x = \{a,\ 0,\ 0,\ 0\}^T$ and $\alpha_1 = v$, $\alpha_2 = \upsilon$, and CORDIC algorithm (9) with $x = \{c,\ 0\}^T$ and $\alpha = \varphi$ can be used in parallel. As a result we have $y_{1n} = kk_hX$, $y_{2n} = -kk_hY$, and for (9) we have $y_{2n} = k_hZ$.

3. Jacobi's method: KP-algorithms can be used for implementation of Jacobi's method to solve an eigenvalue problem (**EVD**) or singular value decomposition (**SVD**) [12,13]. For a given real *(N×N)* matrix **A** they generate a transformation matrix T as a sequence of transformations: $T = \prod_r T_r$. With a proper choice of T_r matrix $A' = T^{-1}AT$ is diagonal with elements equaled to eigenvalues of **A**. In general case, this method uses both circular and hyperbolic rotations and matrices T_r are selected as products RS [13]. The matrices R and S differ from identities accordingly by elements: $r_{pp} = r_{qq} = cos\ \varphi$, $r_{pq} = -r_{qp} = -\ sin\ \varphi$, $s_{pp} = s_{qq} = cosh\ \varphi$, $s_{pq} = s_{qp} = -\ sinh\ \varphi$. Pairs *(p, q) (p<q)* are taken on each pitch of iteration *r* by cyclical exhaustive search. The matrices R and S are selected to annul the elements a_{pq} and a_{qp} of a matrix $A_{r+1} = T_r^{-1}A_rT_r = S^{-1}R^{-1}A_rRS$. Transformation on each pitch of iteration *r* can be replaced by two sequential transformations:

$$B_r = R^{-1}A_rR,\quad A_{r+1} = S^{-1}B_rS. \tag{98}$$

The first transformation should annul the sum $(b_{pq}+b_{qp})$ of elements of matrix B_r, and second - either $(a_{pq}-a_{qp})$ or $(a_{pp}-a_{qq})$ of matrix A_{r+1} .

Let us construct vectors with the following components of A_r, A_{r+1} and B_r:

$$\mathbf{a}_r = (a_{pp}^{(r)},\ a_{pq}^{(r)},\ a_{qp}^{(r)},\ a_{qq}^{(r)})^T,\quad \mathbf{b}_r = (b_{pp}^{(r)},\ b_{pq}^{(r)},\ b_{qp}^{(r)},\ b_{qq}^{(r)})^T\ ,$$
$$\mathbf{a}_{r+1} = (a_{pp}^{(r+1)},\ a_{pq}^{(r+1)},\ a_{qp}^{(r+1)},\ a_{qq}^{(r+1)})^T$$

Using the second property of KP we can exchange (81) with the following:

$$b_r = (R^{-1} \otimes R^T)a_r, \quad a_{r+1} = (S^{-1} \otimes S^T)b_r \qquad (99)$$

These transformations can be calculated in roughly the same time as standard 2-D CORDIC-processor calculates one-side rotation.

For the first transformation we can use algorithm (85) in vectoring mode, if $x=a_r$ and $\xi_{1i}= \xi_{2i}=sign\ (y_{2i}+y_{3i})$, then the result is $y_n=k^2 b_r$. For the second one let's present the matrix S from (8) as a matrix product of elementary hyperbolic rotations: $k_h S = \prod_{i=1}^{n} C_i$.

Then the second transformation from (99) can be presented as:

$$k_h^2 a_{r+1} = \left(\prod_{i=1}^{n} (C_i^{-1} \otimes C_i^T) \right) b_r.$$

New KP-algorithm for implementation of the second transformation can be expressed as:

$$
\begin{pmatrix} b_{pp} \\ b_{pq} \\ b_{qp} \\ b_{qq} \end{pmatrix}_{i+1}
=
\begin{pmatrix}
1 & -\gamma_i & \gamma_i & -\gamma_i^2 \\
-\gamma_i & 1 & -\gamma_i^2 & \gamma_i \\
\gamma_i & -\gamma_i^2 & 1 & -\gamma_i \\
-\gamma_i^2 & \gamma_i & -\gamma_i & 1
\end{pmatrix}
\begin{pmatrix} b_{pp} \\ b_{pq} \\ b_{qp} \\ b_{qq} \end{pmatrix}_{i}
$$
$$\gamma_i = \xi_i 2^{-i}; \quad \xi_i = sign(b_{pqi} - b_{qpi})sign(b_{ppi} - b_{qqi});$$
$$i = 1,2,3,4,4,5...,13,13,14,...,n; \quad b_1 = b_r. \qquad (100)$$

The resultant of the algorithm (60) is $b_n= k_h^2 a_{r+1}$. Following [6,19] to guaranty the convergence of the algorithm (100) an additional condition must be met:

$$arctanh\ (b_{max}/b_{min}) \le \sum_{i=1,2,3,4,45...}^{n} 2\Delta\varphi_i ,$$

where b_{max} and b_{min} extreme positive values of b_r components, $\Delta\varphi_i=arctanh\ 2^{-i}$. Using the second property of KP, one can exchange (99) with the following:

$$b_r = (R^{-1} \otimes R^T)a_r, \quad a_{r+1} = (S^{-1} \otimes S^T)b_r. \qquad (101)$$

It is worth to mention that, for all of the above applications, if CORDIC-processor was used for the implementation, one would need at least two rotations in sequence.

Therefore, our approach can reduce the latency twice through parallel implementation of rotations.

8. Fast Hardware-oriented Algorithm for Quaternion Valued Matrix Decomposition

Parallel implementation of matrix eigenvalue and singular value decompositions is based on triangular arrays with m processors per side, e.g. [10]. Each processor performs a Givens transformation for 2-D vector with either real, or complex, or quaternion elements. The diagonal processors execute CORDIC evaluations and each sends the evaluated control signs to the processors in the same row. As soon as the control signs are available, the off-diagonal processors perform the CORDIC applications.

For example, we can consider a single row of such triangle processor array ($m=8$) to eliminate off-diagonal elements of the first column in either 8×2 quaternion matrix, or 8×4 complex matrix, or 8×8 real matrix as follows:

$$A_{8x2} = \begin{pmatrix} X\ X... & X \\ 0\ X... & X \end{pmatrix}_{\leftrightarrow} \quad A_{8x4} = \begin{pmatrix} X & X... & X & X \\ 0 & X... & X & X \\ 0 & X... & X & X \\ 0 & X... & X & X \end{pmatrix}_{\leftrightarrow} \quad A^{(n)} = \begin{bmatrix} a'_{11} & a'_{12} & ... & a'_{18} \\ 0 & a'_{22} & ... & a'_{28} \\ & ... & ... & \\ 0 & a'_{82} & ... & a'_{88} \end{bmatrix} \quad (102)$$

If control signs are determined by (66) for 2-D quaternion vector $Y_i = [Q_1, Q_2]^T = A_{1(i)} = [a_{11(i)}, a_{21(i)}, a_{31(i)}, a_{41(i)}, a_{51(i)}, a_{61(i)}, a_{71(i)}, a_{81(i)}]^T$, to get this result we use the 8-D CORDIC algorithm:

$$A_{(i+1)} = R_{8,i} A_{(i)}, (i = 0,1,...,n; A_0=A) \quad (103)$$

To get the result (102) with 4-D CORDIC processor array three steps of nulling are necessary. As for 2-D CORDIC processor array we need 7 steps. Table 2 displays the result of area–time comparison.

TABLE 2

Area–Time Comparison for Processor Arrays

CORDIC processor array	2-D CORDIC	4-D Quaternion	8-D Octonion
Number of rotations	56	24	8
Area of processor in terms of 2-D modules	1	2	4
Area of processor array in terms of 2-D modules	8	16	32
Latency (propagation delay time)	$7T_{2D}$	$3T_{4D}$	T_{8D}
Area-time product criteria	$56T_{2D}$	$48T_{4D}$	$32T_{8D}$

The comparison demonstrates that the pipelined implementation with the proposed processor architecture has a 43% decrease in the area-time product and 7 times decrease in running time than that of the 2-D CORDIC implementation if $T_{8D}\cong T_{2D}$. Taking into account (67) these decreases are (38/32) $\cong 1.2$ times less.

Quaternion Jacobi Transformation. The Jacobi procedure problem is as follows. We are given a 2×2 block of a Hermitian quaternion matrix *A*:

$$A_{rc} = \begin{bmatrix} a_{rr} & a_{rc} \\ a_{cr} & a_{cc} \end{bmatrix}, \tag{104}$$

where $a_{cr} = \bar{a}_{rc}$ and diagonal elements are real. The over bar denotes (complex or quaternion) conjugation. In [18], it was shown that a quaternion Jacobi rotation is analogous to a complex Jacobi rotation.

Using a 2×2 unitary quaternion matrix P we can perform a Jacobi rotation on A_{rc}, i.e.

$$P^* A_{rc} P = R_{rc}, \tag{105}$$

where $*$ stands for conjugation-transposition and R_{rc} is a 2×2 quaternion diagonal matrix with real components only:

$$R_{rc} = \begin{bmatrix} r_{rr} & 0 \\ 0 & r_{cc} \end{bmatrix} \tag{106}$$

A general 2×2 unitary quaternion matrix P has elements which have modules that are cosines and sines of some angle θ:

$$P = \begin{bmatrix} c & s \\ -\bar{s} & \bar{c} \end{bmatrix} \tag{107}$$

with $|c| = \cos\theta, |s| = \sin\theta$ and the constraint $c\bar{c} + s\bar{s} = 1$. The elements (real c and quaternion s) can be calculated as following [19]:

$$\tau = \cot 2\theta = \frac{a_{cc} - a_{rr}}{2|a_{rc}|}; \quad c = \cos\theta = \frac{1}{\sqrt{1 + t^2}}; \tag{108}$$

$$t = \frac{sign\tau}{|\tau| + \sqrt{1 + \tau^2}}; \quad s = a_{rc}\frac{\sin\theta}{|a_{rc}|}; \quad \sin\theta = tc$$

Two-sided rotation (105) can be executed with two 8-D rotations in sequence but the angle θ of rotation must be calculated before. This angle can be represented in no evident form (in an *implicit* fashion [20]) as a sequence of sets of control signs $\{\alpha_i \ldots \rho_i\}_\theta, (i = \overline{0, n})$. In general, to calculate an angle $\theta = \arctan y/x$ we can apply algorithm (5) in vectoring mode with quaternion vector $X = [x, y]^T$ and the corresponding sequence will be generated. If we take $x = a_{cc} - a_{rr}$ and $y = a_{cr} + \overline{a_{rc}}$ we can calculate a sequence of sets $\{\alpha_i \ldots \rho_i\}_{2\theta}, (i = \overline{0, n})$ corresponding to angle 2θ.

To determine the angle θ we can transform the corresponding sequence using a formula:

$$tan\ \alpha/2 = \frac{sin\ \alpha}{1 + cos\ \alpha} \tag{109}$$

First, we apply the sequence of sets $\{\alpha_i \ldots \rho_i\}_{2\theta}$ to rotate an unit vector $X = [1, 0, 0, 0, 0, 0, 0, 0]^T$ to get two quaternion components with $|c| = \cos 2\theta, |s| = \sin 2\theta$ in the result $Y = [c, s]^T$ and then we use vectoring mode for modified vector:

$$X = [c + 1, s]^T \tag{110}$$

As a result, we will get a sequence of sets $\{\alpha_i \ldots \rho_i\}_\theta, (i = \overline{0, n})$ corresponding to angle θ. This sequence can be used for orthogonal transformation of matrix A.

To speed up the considered calculations we can use Two Plane Rotation (TPR) method to perform 2×2 SVD as two rotations in parallel [12], [20]. This method represents 2×2 matrix (104) as a sum:

$$A_{rc} = A_1 + A_2 = \begin{bmatrix} p_1 & -q_1 \\ q_1 & p_1 \end{bmatrix} + \begin{bmatrix} -p_2 & q_2 \\ q_2 & p_2 \end{bmatrix}, \tag{111}$$

where

$$p_1 = (a_{rr} + a_{cc})/2, \quad q_1 = (a_{cr} - \overline{a_{rc}})/2,$$
$$p_2 = (a_{cc} - a_{rr})/2, \quad q_2 = (a_{cr} + \overline{a_{rc}})/2.$$

In general case, the transformation (105) can be executed as two rotations in vectoring mode for vectors $X_1 = (p_1, q_1)^T$ and $X_2 = (p_2, q_2)^T$. As a result, they calculate the matrix R_{rc} as:

$$R_{rc} = \begin{bmatrix} y_{11} - y_{21} & 0 \\ 0 & y_{11} + y_{21} \end{bmatrix}, \tag{112}$$

where y_{11} and y_{21} are the first components of the resulting vectors Y_1 and Y_2 correspondently. In addition, two sequences of sets $\{\alpha_i \dots \rho_i\}_{2\theta}, (i = \overline{0, n})$ corresponding to angles $2\theta_1$ and $2\theta_2$ are produced. Then they use two angles $\theta_+ = \theta_1 + \theta_2$ and $\theta_- = \theta_2 - \theta_1$ to modify off-diagonal elements of A in selected rows and columns.

Actually, for Hermitian matrices we have $q_1 = 0$ and the first rotation is unnecessary ($\theta_1 = 0$, $y_{11} = p_1$, and $\theta_+ = \theta_- = \theta_2$). The elements p_1 and p_2 are real and $q_2 = \overline{a_{rc}}$ is a quaternion. Therefore, we can use sets $\{\alpha_i \dots \rho_i\}_{2\theta}, (i = \overline{0, n})$ corresponding to angle $2\theta_2$ to rotate an unit vector for generating vector (70). Then we can get the sequence of sets $\{\alpha_i \dots \rho_i\}_{\theta}, (i = \overline{0, n})$ corresponding to angle θ_2, which is used for orthogonal transformation of $m \times m$ matrix A.

SVD Processor Array. The array is used to implement the Algorithm JA:

1	Algorithm JA ($A^{(0)}=A$)
2	While $\dfrac{S_1^{(s)}}{S_2^{(s)}} > \varepsilon$ {
3	For(all r, c) { -- for all index pairs
4	$$A^{(s+1)} = P^{(s)*}A^{(s)}P^{(s)}$$
5	} –end for
6	} –end while

where S_1-sum of off-diagonal modulus of $A^{(s)}$ in sweep s, S_2-sum of on-diagonal modulus of $A^{(s)}$ in sweep s. We assume that the index pairs (r, c) are chosen cyclic-by-row.

Parallel implementation of $m{\times}m$ matrix singular value decomposition is based on square BLV systolic array with $m/2$ processor elements (PE) per side, where each processor contains one $2{\times}2$ submatrix, e.g. [20]. Taking into account the equality $a_{cr} = \bar{a}_{rc}$ and $\theta_+ = \theta_- = \theta_2$ for Hermitian matrix we can use a triangle processor array with one diagonal PE and (m-2) off-diagonal PEs per horizontal side, and one diagonal PE and ($m/2$-1) off-diagonal PEs per vertical side. The configuration of this array to zero matrix element a_{12} is shown in Figure 23 as an example.

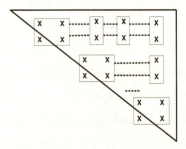

Fig.23. Triangle processor array for Jacobi SVD.

Fig.24. Octonion CORDIC application.

Fig.25. Octonion CORDIC evaluation.

In Figure 24 and Figure 25 an Octonion CORDIC application and evaluation symbols are shown correspondently. Each diagonal PE performs a Jacobi transformation for 2×2 matrix with quaternion elements. It consists of 2 OCA modules [10] (OCA_1 and OCA_3) to execute CORDIC evaluations (see Figure 26) and one module OCA_2 to rotate vector $X= [1, 0, 0, 0, 0, 0, 0, 0]^T$ to get two quaternion components in the result $Y= [c, s]^T$.

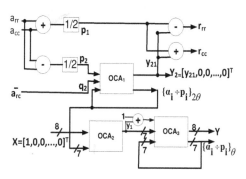

Fig.26. Diagonal PE of the SVD array.

This result is used to calculate vector (110) for module OCA_3 to generate evaluated control signs $\{\alpha_i \dots \rho_i\}_\theta, (i = \overline{0, n})$ and to send them to the off-diagonal PEs in the same row on-the-fly. As soon as the control signs are available, the off-diagonal processors perform the CORDIC applications for 2-D quaternion vector as it shown in Figure 24. A phase of internal rearrangement of the elements of A_{rc} must be made after each iteration, and also transference between submatrices of such form that locate in the diagonal submatrices the elements to be annulled. It is important to stress that the diagonal of resulting quaternion matrix has real components only.

Error Analysis and Simulation Results. Following [17] and [21] we can analyze two types of quantization error: an approximation error due to the quantized representation of rotation angle and a rounding error due to the finite precision representation in fixed point arithmetic.

For fixed point arithmetic, all numbers have to be restricted to -1< x <1. Again, the number possesses h digits and machine accuracy is given by $\varepsilon Fi = 2$-h-1.

If the result of the computation lies within the range, $z = Fi(x \pm y) = x \pm y$ holds. Shift right is calculated with a rounding error according to $z = Fi(x \; op \; y) = x \; op \; y + \varepsilon Fi$.

Therefore, if an error vector [21] in each step due to rounding is $e(i) = [e_{1i}, e_{2i}, e_{3i}, e_{4i}, e_{5i}, e_{6i}, e_{7i}, e_{8i}]^T$, an upper bound for its absolute rounding error is:

$$|e(i)| \leq \sqrt{8} \, \varepsilon_{Fi} = 2\sqrt{2} \, \varepsilon_{Fi} \qquad (113)$$

Rotation angle θ is calculated as a sequence of sets $\{\alpha_i \ldots \rho_i\}_\theta, (i = \overline{0,n})$ with approximation error δ which is bounded by the smallest rotation angle σ. That is,

$$|\delta| \leq \sigma = arctan2^{-n} \qquad (114)$$

The quantization error of an operation of vector rotation is governed by [17]:

$$\tilde{Y} = \left(\prod_{i=0}^{n-1} R_{8,i}\right)X + \sum_{i=0}^{n-1}\left(\prod_{j=i}^{n-1} R_{8,j}\right)e(i) + e(n) \quad (115)$$

Scaling correction introduces an additive error [21]):

$$\hat{Y} = (1/k)\tilde{Y} + E\varepsilon_{Fi},$$

where $E = [1, 1, 1, 1, 1, 1, 1, 1]^{\mathrm{T}}$.

Taking into account (113), the worst bound of (115) can be found with [21],

$$\left\| k\hat{Y} - \left(\prod_{i=0}^{n-1} R_{8,i}\right)X \right\|_2 \leq 2\sqrt{2}\varepsilon_{Fi}G(n), \quad (116)$$

where

$$G(n) = \left(1 + \sum_{i=0}^{n-1} \prod_{j=i}^{n-1}\|R_{8j}\|_2\right) = 1 + \sum_{i=0}^{n-1} \prod_{j=i}^{n-1} \sqrt{1 + 7*2^{-2j}} \quad (117)$$

For $m \times m$ matrices A and P the 2-norm of the absolute error of one sweep of SVD calculation is given [25] by:

$$\left\| A^{(s)} - P^{(s)*}A^{(0)}P^{(s)} \right\|_2 \leq \sqrt{2}\varepsilon_{Fi}G(n)\sqrt{(2m-4)}m(m-1) \quad (118)$$

and an overall error for p sweeps holds:

$$\left\| A - P^*A^{(0)}P \right\|_2 \leq p\varepsilon_{Fi}G(n)\sqrt{(2m-4)}m(m-1)/2, \quad (119)$$

where A – resulting diagonal matrix containing eigenvalues of A.

Simulation was executed using C# in Visual Studio 2010, .NET Framework 4.0 environment. Figure 27 illustrates the evaluation mode of OCA (Figure 9) as an average result of $\log_{10}\left(\sum_{j=2}^{8}|y_{ji}|/|y_{1j}|\right)$ for 100 pairs of quaternions with random elements in range ±10 where yji denotes the jth component of a vector Y_i at the beginning of the $(i+1)$th iteration.

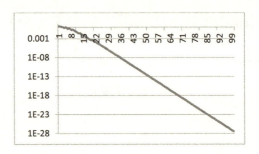

Fig.27. Accuracy $\log_{10}\left(\sum_{j=2}^{8}|y_{ji}|/|y_{1i}|\right)$ of OCA evaluation vs. number of

iterations (i).

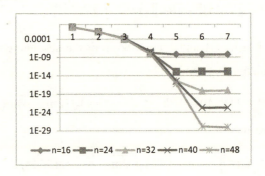

Fig.28. Quality of diagonalization $\log_{10}(S_1/S_2)$ vs. number of sweeps (s).

Following [20] there were taken 1000 random Hermitian 15×15 quaternion matrices for decomposition. In Figure 28 the diagonalization results are shown as an average value of $\log_{10}(S_1/S_2)$ for n=16, 24, 32, 40, and 48.

9. Hardware-oriented Encryption Algorithms with Hyper-complex Number Systems

There are two hyper-complex number systems which are used in modern encryption systems: quaternions and octonions [8]. The application of the quaternion number system is attractive in computation models due to its matrix representation. It has been applied as a mathematical model in encryption by several researchers. In [22]-[24], a new quaternion encryption scheme (QES) is proposed for signal encryption providing good hiding properties.

Recently in [26], [27], new encryption schemes based on non-associative octonion algebra were proposed for signal encryption with better security against lattice attack and/or more capability for protocol design.

Hyper-complex number based ciphers are attractive not only because they may be represented using matrix-vector multiplication but also that the inverse matrix for such transformation is a transpose of the original matrix. Matrix operations are rather simple and can be efficiently implemented that is especially important for multimedia data transmission.

The QES works as follows. A sequence of signal samples is arranged as a sequence of frames containing three three-component vectors, represented as a 3x3 matrix B, i-th column B_i of which is the i-th mentioned above sample-vector ($i = \overline{1,3}$). Each vector B_i in a frame is encrypted by applying to it one and the same transformation represented by its multiplication from one side by some quaternion q and from the other side by its inverse q^{-1} producing the ciphertext vector B_i'

$$B_i' = q^{-1} B_i q, i = \overline{1,3}, \tag{120}$$

or, in the terms of plaintext-ciphertext matrices, (120) may be rewritten as

$$B' = q^{-1}Bq , \tag{121}$$

where $B' = (B'_1, B'_2, B'_3)$. Transformation (121) may be also represented using matrix multiplication of the plaintext matrix B by a secret key matrix depending on q and producing the ciphertext matrix B'.

QES details .The quaternion q is a hyper complex number represented by

$$q = w + xi + yj + zk = (w, V) , \tag{122}$$

where w, x, y, z are real numbers, (i, j, k) forms an orthonormal basis in R^3, $V = xi + yj + zk$,

$$i^2 = j^2 = k^2 = ijk = -1 . \tag{123}$$

Inverse q^{-1} of the quaternion q is a quaternion such that

$$q^{-1}q = qq^{-1} = 1 , \tag{124}$$

and

$$q^{-1} = \frac{w - xi - yj - zk}{|q|^2} = \frac{(w, -V)}{|q|^2} , \tag{125}$$

Where

$$|q| = \sqrt{w^2 + x^2 + y^2 + z^2} \tag{126}$$

is the norm of q. Vector transform (80) is rotation if $|q| = 1$, and may be represented as a matrix-vector product

$$B'_i = \Gamma(q)B_i , i = \overline{1,3} , \tag{127}$$

where

$$\Gamma(q) = \frac{1}{|q|^2} \begin{bmatrix} |q|^2 - 2(y^2 + z^2) & 2(xy + wz) & 2(xz - wy) \\ 2(xy - wz) & |q|^2 - 2(x^2 + z^2) & 2(yz + wx) \\ 2(xz + wy) & 2(yz - wx) & |q|^2 - 2(x^2 + y^2) \end{bmatrix} . \tag{128}$$

Equation (127) may be written similar to (121) as

$$B' = \Gamma(q)B \, .$$

(129)

Plaintext matrix B can be restored from (129) using (128)

$$B = (\Gamma(q))^{-1} B' \, ,$$

(130)

where $(\Gamma(q))^{-1}$ is the inverse of $\Gamma(q)$, i.e.

$$(\Gamma(q))^{-1}\Gamma(q) = \Gamma(q)(\Gamma(q))^{-1} = E \, ,$$

(131)

where E is 3×3 unity matrix such that $e_{ij} = \begin{cases} 1, i = j \\ 0, i \neq j \end{cases}$; note that $(\Gamma(q))^{-1} = \Gamma(q)'$, where x' is a transpose of the matrix x. The QES assumes that each next frame is enciphered using another quaternion, three vector v components (x,y,z) of which are obtained as three row elements of the matrix (128) used for encryption of the previous frame whereas its scalar component $,w$, is set to zero, that is

$$q_m = \begin{cases} w + xi + yj + zk, m = 0 \\ 0 + x_m i + y_m j + z_m k, m > 0 \end{cases},$$

(132)

where $x_m = (\Gamma(q_{m-1}))_{11}, y_m = (\Gamma(q_{m-1}))_{12}, z_m = (\Gamma(q_{m-1}))_{13}, m > 0$, and the key matrix used for the m-th frame is $\Gamma(q_m)$. The next quaternion components may be taken not from the first row as shown above but from the other rows of the matrix (128) as well, or from its columns. Hence, encryption algorithm [22]-[24] uses dynamically changing matrices of the form (128) in (129), (130) that are claimed to allow increasing its security contrary to the usage of static matrix (128).

It was expected that QES provides high security due to using dynamic key matrix obtained by changing the next quaternion components. But, this algorithm is a particular case of the well-known Hill cipher (HC) [28]. The HC is susceptible to the known plaintext-ciphertext attack (KPCA), therefore QES can be broken with the KPCA, and the secret key matrix can be obtained. It was shown in [29] that QES is susceptible to KPCA due to not proper choice of the frame size and the procedure of secret quaternion updating. To improve QES security, we propose a QES modification (M-QES) resistant to the KPCA by adjusting the frame size and the quaternion update procedure. In addition, hardware-oriented implementation of the QES modification (HW-QES) is proposed based on the ideas from [25], [30].

QES modification (M-QES). As it was shown, the weakness of QES follows from the use of the frame having nine samples comprising a 3×3 matrix with a non-zero determinant in the general case. If to reduce the frame size to less than nine samples (say six, or three), and change the key matrix for each new frame as proposed in QES, then there is no opportunity to apply the known plaintext-ciphertext attack due to the number of unknowns (nine) is greater than the number of equations (six, or three) and the opponent does not have enough equations to solve such equations now. But due to (132), actually all the key matrices starting from the second one are built using only three-component quaternion (122), and even using a three-component vector as a plaintext, the opponent is able to find three unknowns from three equations if he has the plaintext-ciphertext pair. Hence, to counter this line of attack, additionally, modified QES shall not use (132) for getting the next key matrix from the previous one, but it uses a similar procedure with four quaternion components. Such an opportunity is mentioned in [22]-[24] but it was not considered as an important. That's why, the way of producing the next key matrix may be as follows

$$q_m = \begin{cases} w + xi + yj + zk, m = 0 \\ w_m + x_m i + y_m j + z_m k, m > 0 \end{cases}, \tag{133}$$

where $w_m = (\Gamma(q_{m-1}))_{31}$, $x_m = (\Gamma(q_{m-1}))_{12}$, $y_m = (\Gamma(q_{m-1}))_{23}$, $z_m = (\Gamma(q_{m-1}))_{13}, m > 0$, and the key matrix used for the m-th plaintext vector is $\Gamma(q_m)$. In such a case, the key matrix is defined by four numbers specified in (133), and using three equations from the known plaintext-ciphertext pair, it is not possible to determine them uniquely: there is one free parameter on which all other values depend. The number of possible variants of such a matrix is defined by the number of possible values of the free parameter. In the case of the use of n-byte float point numbers, this number is equal to 2^{8n}, e.g., if $n=4$, then this number is 2^{32} that does not provide enough cryptographic strength. If one plaintext vector is subjected to l subsequent such kind transformations then an opponent sees results only after l iterations, and he is not able to have a matrix depending on a quaternion providing transformation from input to output. He can work in that direction trying to determine all quaternions used but each matrix depends of 4 numbers and there are l such matrices hence number of parameters is $4l$ and number of equations is 3. Hence number of free unknowns is $4l$-3 that is equal to 1 only in the case of $l=1$. For $l=2$, it is 5 and with $n=4$ it yields already $2^{8nl}=2^{160}$ variants. If the opponent tries just to find a matrix providing total transformation, he faces a problem with 9 unknowns and 3 equations; hence he has 6 free unknowns that results in 2^{192} variants. Hence, with $l=2$, we have secure encryption with search space of 2^{160} variants at least.

Thus far the proposed QES modification, M-QES, is as follows:

1. Each plaintext three-component vector Pi is subjected to l subsequent transformations (127), where quaternion q_m and its transformation matrix $\Gamma(q_m)$ are defined by (133) and (128) respectively, m=0,1,.. resulting in the ciphertext vector c_i :

$$D_{il} = P_i,$$
$$D_{il+m+1} = \Gamma(q_{il+m})D_{il+m}, m = \overline{0,l-1}$$
$$C_i = D_{(i+1)l}, i = 0,1,..$$

2. Decryption is performed as follows

$$D_{(i+1)l} = C_i,$$
$$D_{il+m-1} = \Gamma(q_{il+m})'D_{il+m}, m = l, l-1,..,1$$
$$P_i = D_{il}, i = 0,1,..$$

Note that, to overcome zero to zero mapping, we XOR (bit-by-bit exclusive OR operation) the plaintext components with the quaternion elements and then we perform encryption. Note also that instead of the use of (133), to get the next quaternion defining the next transformation matrix and defined by the previous transformation matrix, a pseudo-random number generator can be used with the seed value known to both the sender and receiver of the transferred text.

Hardware-oriented QES (HW-QES). To simplify implementation of the transform (127) used in QES and its modification, M-QES, we can use the quaternion $d = w + t(xi + yj + zk)$ where $w^2 = \dot{x}^2 + y^2 + z^2$, $t = 2^{-i}$, to form matrix (128) with

$$w = 2^m + 1, m = 2k + 1, x = 2^{m-i}\alpha, y = 2^{\frac{m+1}{2}-i}\beta, z = 2^{-i}\gamma,$$
$$|d|^2 = (2^m + 1)^2(1 + 2^{-2i}), \alpha, \beta, \gamma \in \{-1,1\}, K > k \geq 0,$$
$$|i| < I$$
(134)

as follows:

$$\Gamma(d) =$$
$$= \frac{1}{|d|^2}\begin{bmatrix} (2^m+1)^2 + 2^{2m-2i} - 2^{m+1-2i} - 2^{-2i} & \alpha\beta2^{3(m+1)/2-2i} + \gamma(2^{m-i+1} + 2^{-i+1}) & \alpha\gamma2^{m-2i+1} - \beta(2^m+1)2^{(m+3)/2-i} \\ \alpha\beta2^{3(m+1)/2-2i} - \gamma(2^{m-i+1} + 2^{-i+1}) & (2^m+1)^2 + 2^{m+1-2i} - 2^{2m-2i} - 2^{-2i} & \beta\gamma2^{(m+3)/2-2i} + \alpha2^{-i+m+1}(2^m+1) \\ \alpha\gamma2^{m-2i+1} + \beta(2^m+1)2^{(m+3)/2-i} & \beta\gamma2^{(m+3)/2-2i} - \alpha2^{-i+m+1}(2^m+1) & (2^m+1)^2 + 2^{-2i} - 2^{2m-2i} - 2^{m+1-2i} \end{bmatrix}$$
(135)

Entries of the matrix (135) are integers if $i<0$. Let's consider plaintext signal and transformation (135) having values from Z_N, where $N=2^n$. In such a case all operations are done modulo 2^n. Division by square of the norm in (135) is correct since according to (134) square of the norm is an odd number having multiplicative inverse modulo 2^n. As far as entries of (135) contain contributors being powers of two, when these powers exceed n, they vanish modulo 2^n, and matrix (135) degenerates to the unity matrix not providing hiding of the plaintext. To avoid the matrix degeneration, we require not vanishing of entries in (135) modulo 2^n:

$$\min(2m - 2i, m + 1 - 2i, -2i) < n$$
$$\min(3(m + 1)/2 - 2i, m - i + 1, -i + 1) < n$$
$$\min(m - 2i + 1, 3(m + 1)/2 - i, (m + 3)/2 - i) < n$$
$$\min((m + 3)/2 - 2i, 2m - i + 1, m - i + 1) < n$$

(136)

Since $m > 0, i < 0$,

$$2m \geq m + 1, -2i \geq -i + 1.$$

(137)

Hence, from (136), (137), one gets

$$-2i < n,$$
$$(m + 3)/2 - i < n.$$
$$m - i + 1 < n$$

(138)

From (134) and (138), one gets

$$-2i < n,$$
$$2k + 2 - i < n.$$

(139)

For example, if $n=8$, i may take values of -1, -2, -3, and k may take values 0, 1, 2 for $i=-1$; 0, 1 for $i=-2$; and 0, 1 for $i=-3$. If $n=8$, $i=-3$, $k=1$, then the matrix (135) is as follows

$$\Gamma(d) = \frac{1}{|d|^2} \begin{bmatrix} (2^3 + 1)^2 + 2^{12} - 2^{10} - 2^6 \alpha\beta 2^{12} + \gamma(2^7 + 2^4) & \alpha\gamma 2^{10} - \beta(2^3 + 1)2^6 \\ \alpha\beta 2^{12} - \gamma(2^7 + 2^4) & (2^3 + 1)^2 + 2^{10} - 2^{12} - 2^6 \beta\gamma 2^9 + \alpha 2^7 (2^3 + 1) \\ \alpha\gamma 2^{10} + \beta(2^3 + 1)2^6 & \beta\gamma 2^9 - \alpha 2^7 (2^3 + 1) & (2^3 + 1)^2 + 2^6 - 2^{12} - 2^{10} \end{bmatrix}$$

$$= \frac{1}{(2^3 + 1)^2 (1 + 2^6)} \begin{bmatrix} (2^3 + 1)^2 - 2^6 & \gamma(2^7 + 2^4) & -\beta 2^6 \\ -\gamma(2^7 + 2^4) & (2^3 + 1)^2 - 2^6 & \alpha 2^7 \\ \beta 2^6 & -\alpha 2^7 & (2^3 + 1)^2 + 2^6 \end{bmatrix} \mod 2^8$$

The transform (127) may be implemented with matrix (135) very fast (without the division by the quadratic norm) using simple shift-add operations. Compensation of the scaling factor may be executed with hardware once after l such transformations using a product:

$$P = \frac{1}{\prod\limits_{j=1}^{l}(2^{m_j}+1)^2(1+2^{-2i_j})} \, ,$$

where m_j, i_j are the values m, i for the j-th consecutive transformation.

The hardware-oriented (HW-QES), is based on the use of (136) and is similar to M-QES. HW-QES is defined as follows:

Each plaintext three-component vector P is subjected to l subsequent transformations (127) (quaternion $q=d$ and its transformation matrix $\Gamma(q)$ are defined by (134) and (135) respectively, m=0,1,..), resulting in the ciphertext vector C_i:

$$D_{tl} = P_t,$$
$$D_{tl+m+1} = \Gamma(q_{tl+m})D_{tl+m}, m = \overline{0, l-1},$$
$$C_t = D_{(t+1)l}, t = 0,1,..$$

where q_t is a value of the quaternion d obtained from (134) for some s-th combination of the values of five parameters ($i, k, \alpha, \beta, \gamma$) chosen according to some enumeration procedure (e.g., using pseudo-random number generator with agreed secret seed value).

1. Decryption is performed as follows

$$D_{(t+1)l} = C_t,$$
$$D_{tl+m-1} = \Gamma(q_{tl+m})D_{tl+m}, m = \overline{l, l-1,..,1}$$
$$P_t = D_{tl}, t = 0,1,..$$

Note that, to overcome zero to zero mapping, we XOR (bit-by-bit exclusive OR operation) the plaintext components with the quaternion elements and then we perform encryption. The HW-QES cipher uses dynamically generated transformation matrices number of different variants of which determines cryptographic strength of the cipher. This number is calculated as the number of possible different combinations of the parameters of the set of numbers (134). This set has five parameters: $\alpha, \beta, \gamma \in \{-1,1\}$, $i \in \{-1,-2,-3,...,-I\}$ (we consider only negative values for this parameter to have integer-valued entries of (135)), $k \in \{0,..,K-1\}$; and the numbers are in z_N where $N = 2^n$. Let us estimate the number of possible combinations of these five parameters. Taking into account (139), number of possible variants of i is $\min(\frac{n}{2}-1,I)$, and the number of possible combinations of $(i,\ k)$ is $\min(IK,\sum_{i=1}^{n/2-1}\frac{n-i-2}{2})=\min(IK,(n/2-1)(3n/8-1))$ if $\frac{n}{2}-1\leq I$. The number of combinations of all five parameters is $8\min(IK,(n/2-1)(3n/8-1))$ since α,β,γ are binary. If $n=24$, $I=30$, $K=15$, then the number of combinations is 704. If a plaintext vector is subjected to $l=14$ consecutive transformations, as it is assumed in the M-QES, the number of all possible combinations of the parameters of transformations is $704^{14}\approx10^{40}$ thus providing large cryptographic strength of such a cipher.

OES details. The use of quaternions to represent color images has been introduced by Sangwine [31]. A color image is represented as a pure quaternion image:

$$B(x,y)=0+r(x,y)i+g(x,y)j+b(x,y)k , \qquad (140)$$

where $r(x,y)$, $g(x,y)$, $b(x,y)$ are respectively the red, green and blue components of a pixel at position (x,y) in the image $B(x,y)$. This representation has allowed the definition of powerful tools for color image processing such as Fourier transforms, correlation or edge detection.

The typical matrix operation for an encoding process is an one-sided matrix multiplication of the plaintext matrix B by a secret key matrix M to produce the ciphertext matrix B':

$$B' = M \times B \qquad (141)$$

The plaintext quaternion valued matrix B may be considered as a block-matrix where each block (or frame) consists of two pixels from (140) in form of quaternion valued vector $X=(q1,\ q2)^T$ as a column of B. Then we can describe with matrix M an 8-D rotation of equivalent 8-D real vector $X=(q11, q12, q13, q14, q21, q22, q23, q24)^T$, where quaternion l has components $q_l=(ql1, ql2, ql3, ql4)$ $(l=1,2)$.

There is a natural way to describe an 8-D rotation using octonions. The octonion o is a hyper-complex number represented as

$$o = w + xe_1 + ye_2 + ze_3 + ae_4 + be_5 + ce_6 + de_7 = (w, V)$$ (142)

where w,x,y,z,a,b,c,d are real numbers, e_i $(i=1...7)$ form an orthonormal basis in R^7, $V = (xe_1 + ye_2 + ze_3 + ae_4 + be_5 + ce_6 + de_7)$,

$$e_i^2 = -1, (i = 1..7), e_i e_j = -e_j e_i, e_i e_{i+1} = e_{i+3}$$ (143)

where addition is made modulo 7 (e.g., $e_6 e_7 = e_2$). Inverse o^{-1} of the octonion o is an octonion such that

$$o^{-1}o = oo^{-1} = I,$$ (144)

and

$$o^{-1} = \frac{(w - v)}{|o|^2}$$ (145)

where

$$|o| = \sqrt{w^2 + x^2 + y^2 + z^2 + a^2 + b^2 + c^2 + d^2}$$ (146)

is the norm of o.

If an octonion has a unit norm ($|\square|=1$), it can be represented in "polar" form

$$o = \cos\varphi + \sin\varphi(\alpha e_1 + \beta e_2 + \gamma e_3 + \delta e_4 + \lambda e_5 + \mu e_6 + \rho e_7)$$ (147)

Vector transform with octonion (145) is an 8-D rotation by angle φ, and may be represented as a matrix-vector product [25]

$$B^{'} = \cos\varphi R_{8}B \,, \tag{148}$$

where

$$R_{8} = \begin{pmatrix} 1 & \alpha t & \beta t & \gamma t & \delta t & \lambda t & \mu t & \rho t \\ -\alpha t & 1 & -\delta t & -\rho t & \beta t & -\mu t & \lambda t & \gamma t \\ -\beta t & \delta t & 1 & -\lambda t & -\alpha t & \gamma t & -\rho t & \mu t \\ -\gamma t & \rho t & \lambda t & 1 & -\mu t & -\beta t & \delta t & -\alpha t \\ -\delta t & -\beta t & \alpha t & \mu t & 1 & -\rho t & -\gamma t & \lambda t \\ -\lambda t & \mu t & -\lambda t & \beta t & \rho t & 1 & -\alpha t & -\delta t \\ -\mu t & -\lambda t & \rho t & -\delta t & \gamma t & \alpha t & 1 & -\beta t \\ -\rho t & -\gamma t & -\mu t & \alpha t & -\lambda t & \delta t & \beta t & 1 \end{pmatrix}, \tag{149}$$

and $t = \tan(\varphi)$,

8-D rotation with octonion (142) may be used for encoding (141) as

$$B' = \Gamma(o)B \,, \tag{150}$$

where

$$\Gamma(o) = |o|^{-1} \begin{pmatrix} w & x & y & z & a & b & c & d \\ -x & w & -a & -d & y & -c & b & z \\ -y & a & w & -b & -x & z & -d & c \\ -z & d & b & w & -c & -y & a & -x \\ -a & -y & x & c & w & -d & -z & b \\ -b & c & -z & y & d & w & -x & -a \\ -c & -b & d & -a & z & x & w & -y \\ -d & -z & -c & x & -b & a & y & w \end{pmatrix}, \tag{151}$$

Transform (150) represents multiplication of octonions o and B resulting in octonion B'.

Plaintext vector B can be restored from (150) using (151)

$$B = \Gamma(o)^{-1}B^{'} \,, \tag{152}$$

where $\Gamma(o)^{-1}$ is inverse of $\Gamma(o)$, i.e.

$$\Gamma(o)(\Gamma(o))^{-1} = (\Gamma(o))^{-1}\Gamma(o) = E \,, \tag{153}$$

where E is 8×8 unity matrix such that $e_{ij} = \begin{cases} 1, i = j \\ 0, i \neq j \end{cases}$; note that $(\Gamma(o))^{-1} = (\Gamma(o))^T$,

where X^T is a transpose of the matrix x . The OES assumes that each next 8-component frame is enciphered using another octonion, components (142) of which are obtained from the elements of the matrix (151) used for encryption of the previous frame, for example, by addition of elements of some two rows, i and j, $i, j \in \{1,...8\}, i \neq j$, that is

$$
\begin{aligned}
w_m &= (\Gamma(o_{m-1}))_{i1} + (\Gamma(o_{m-1}))_{j1}, \\
x_m &= (\Gamma(o_{m-1}))_{i2} + (\Gamma(o_{m-1}))_{j2}, \\
&\ldots \\
c_m &= (\Gamma(o_{m-1}))_{i7} + (\Gamma(o_{m-1}))_{j7}, \\
d_m &= (\Gamma(o_{m-1}))_{i8} + (\Gamma(o_{m-1}))_{j8}, m > 0
\end{aligned} \tag{154}
$$

and the key matrix used for the m-th frame is $\Gamma(o_m)$. Values i,j shall be shared by the communicating parties. Contrary to QES (see (133)), we need applying some operations (as shown in (154) or other) to the elements of the previous matrix because otherwise new matrix (151) contains the same (by modulo) elements as the previous one. As far as the matix is defined by 8 elements and the frame size is also 8, such transformation as (150) is susceptible to KPCA, because if the plaintext and ciphertext are known then we may have 8 equations with 8 unknowns which can be uniquely solved. Hence, we need more secret parameters. If a ciphertext is obtained after $l=2$ consecutive applications of (151), then an opponent is to solve a system of nonlinear square equations (because of twice applied (151) coefficients are multiplied) to find 8 octonion components from 8 equations, or to find 64 elements of the matrix resulting after two transformations. In the first case the number of effective unknowns is 8^2, and in the second it is also 64. With 8 equations and 64 unknowns, opponent faces with necessity of enumeration of 56 free unknowns. If each such unknown has 8 values then 2^{168} variants are to be considered that is not feasible.

Hence, OES method may be represented as follows:

Algorithm OES:

Input: P[1],P[2],..., - plaintext, o1 – octonion with 8 components, $l \geq 2$ – number of consecutive iterations (l=2 is default for OES), SN[1..l] – secret integers each having multiplicative inverse

Output: C[1], C[2],..

m=1;o[m]=o1; B=P[1];

While not end of input plaintext{

For (i=1,l){

Calculate $\Gamma(o[m])$ according to (151)

Calculate B' according to (150);

B'=SN[i]·B' + $\Gamma(o[m])_{1,1:8}$;

m++;

Calculate o[m] according to (154), (151);

}

C[m/l]= B';

B=P[m/l+1];

Calculate o[m] according to (154), (151);

}/*end*/

Use of the secret numbers *SN[1..l]* with n binary digits extends key space of the algorithm 2^{ln} times, XOR operation with the first row of the current transformation matrix is used to avoid mapping of zero to zero. Decryption in OES method is straightforward and assumes l times applying of XOR operation, multiplication by inverses of *SN[1..l]*, and applied (152) for each ciphertext block *C[m]*.

So, encryption algorithm uses dynamically changing matrices of the form (151) in (150), (112) for increasing its security contrary to the usage of static matrix (151).

Hardware-oriented OES. To simplify implementation of the transform (151) used in OES we can take the octonion $o = w + t(xe_1 + ye_2 + ze_3 + ae_4 + be_5 + ce_6 + de_7)$, where $x^2 + y^2 + z^2 + a^2 + b^2 + c^2 + d^2 = w^2$ and $t = 2^{-i}$, to form matrix (151) with

$w = 2^m + 1$, $m = 2k$, $x = 2^{m-1}\alpha$,
$y = 2^{m-1}\beta$, $z = 2^{m-1}\gamma$, $a = 2^{m-1}\delta$, $b = 2^{m/2}\lambda$, $c = 2^{m/2}\mu$, $d = \rho$, $|o|^2 = (2^m + 1)^2(1 + 2^{-2i})$, $\alpha, \beta, \gamma, \delta, \lambda, \mu, \rho \in \{-1, 1\}$, $K \geq k > 0, I \geq i \geq -I$, (155)

Obtained from (151), (155) matrix looks as follows (156):

$$
\Gamma(o) = \begin{bmatrix}
2^m + 1 & \alpha 2^{m-1-i} & \beta 2^{m-1-i} & \gamma 2^{m-1-i} & \delta 2^{m-1-i} & \lambda 2^{m/2-i} & \mu 2^{m-1-i} & \rho 2^{-i} \\
-\alpha 2^{m-1-i} & 2^m + 1 & -\delta 2^{m-1-i} & -\rho 2^{-i} & \beta 2^{m-1-i} & -\mu 2^{m-1-i} & \lambda 2^{m/2-i} & \gamma 2^{m-1-i} \\
-\beta 2^{m-1-i} & \delta 2^{m-1-i} & 2^m + 1 & -\lambda 2^{m/2-i} & -\alpha 2^{m-1-i} & \gamma 2^{m-1-i} & -\rho 2^{-i} & \mu 2^{m-1-i} \\
-\gamma 2^{m-1-i} & \rho 2^{-i} & \lambda 2^{m/2-i} & 2^m + 1 & -\mu 2^{m-1-i} & -\beta 2^{m-1-i} & \delta 2^{m-1-i} & -\alpha 2^{m-1-i} \\
-\delta 2^{m/2-i} & -\beta 2^{m-1-i} & \alpha 2^{m-1-i} & \mu 2^{m-1-i} & 2^m + 1 & -\rho 2^{-i} & -\gamma 2^{m-1-i} & \lambda 2^{m/2-i} \\
-\lambda 2^{m/2-i} & \mu 2^{m-1-i} & -\gamma 2^{m-1-i} & \beta 2^{m-1-i} & \rho 2^{-i} & 2^m + 1 & -\alpha 2^{m-1-i} & -\delta 2^{m/2-i} \\
-\mu 2^{m-1-i} & -\lambda 2^{m/2-i} & \rho 2^{-i} & -\delta 2^{m-1-i} & \gamma 2^{m-1-i} & \alpha 2^{m-1-i} & 2^m + 1 & -\beta 2^{m-1-i} \\
-\rho 2^{-i} & -\gamma 2^{m-1-i} & -\mu 2^{m-1-i} & \alpha 2^{m-1-i} & -\lambda 2^{m/2-i} & \delta 2^{m/2-i} & \beta 2^{m-1-i} & 2^m + 1
\end{bmatrix}
$$

Hence, method HW-OES is the same as OES but octonions are generated now not by (154) but by (156) (all appearances of (154) shall be replaced by (156) in Algorithm OES description) using a pseudo-random number generator with the specified seed value shared by the sender and receiver. Initial octonion *O1* used in OES is also obtained by (156) using the pseudo-random number generator. If a plaintext is represented as integers from Z_N, as for image processing where

$N=256$, then all operations are to be done modulo N, including calculation of the square root according to (146), (111). If $N=2^n$, norm (106) must be invertible modulo N because of division used in (151). According to (155), the norm is an odd number, and, hence its inverse exists. From the other side, the norm needs square root operation. According to (155), the square root (146) exists and

$$|o| = (2^m + 1) \bmod 2^n \tag{157}$$

for

$$i \le -n/2. \tag{158}$$

The HW-OES cipher uses dynamically generated transformation matrices (156) (with the norm (157)) number of different variants of which determines cryptographic strength of the cipher. This number is calculated as the number of possible different combinations of the parameters of the set of numbers (155). This set has nine parameters: $\alpha, \beta, \gamma, \delta, \lambda, \mu, \rho \in \{-1,1\}$, $i \in \{-n/2,..,-1\}$, (we consider only negative values for this parameter to have integer-valued entries of (151), (156) and take into account (158)), $k \in \{1,..,K\}$; and the numbers are in Z_N where $N = 2^n$. The number of combinations of all the nine parameters is $2^7(I - n/2 + 1)K$. If $I=32$, $K=32$, then the number of combinations is $O(2^{16})$. If $n=32$, then number of values for each element from $SN[1..l]$ is 2^{32}, and the number of variants is $O(2^{48})$. For OES, $l=2$, and hence the key space is $O(2^{48l}) = O(2^{96})$ that corresponds to a strong enough cipher. We can further increase its security using $l>2$.

11. Conclusion

In this study, novel CORDIC-like algorithms were presented for multi-dimensional DLT. Thus, matrix computations can be sped up by expressing them in terms of higher dimensional rotations. The area–time comparison demonstrated an appreciable improvement with the proposed new processor architectures over the 2-D and 4-D CORDIC implementations. These powerful algorithms can be used for matrix triangularization, QRD, SVD, and other important matrix decompositions. It allows to increase the level of parallelism of a system, and improves the speed of CORDIC-processor arrays by a maximum of seven times, in contrast to the 2-D CORDIC-processor array. It's crucial to mention that all improvements over the basic CORDIC processor (scaling iterations, redundant arithmetic, high-radix arithmetic, etc. [2]) may be incorporated in the offered processors as well.

Processors with hardware implementation of this algorithm can be fruitful in many signal-processing problems requiring lots of parallel computations.

REFERENCES

1. J.E Volder, "The CORDIC Trigonometric Computing Technique." *IEEE Trans. On Electronic Computers*, vol. EC-9, pp. 227-231, 1960.

2. P. Meher, J. Valls, T.-B., Juang, K. Sridharan, K. Maharatna, "50 Years of CORDIC: Algorithms, Architectures and Applications", *IEEE Trans. on Circuits and Systems I: Regular Papers*, Vol. 56, no. 9, pp. 893 – 1907, Sept. 2009

3. S. Walter, "A Unified Algorithm for Elementary Functions," In Proc. of Spring Joint Computer Conf., 1971, pp. 379-385.

4. E. Doukhnitch "One Way to Execute Digital Linear Transform", *Kibernetica* (Cybernetics and Systems Analysis), No5, Kiev, May 1982, pp.96-98

5. E.I. Doukhnitch. Two Generalized Algorithms of Discrete Linear Transforms, Coll. Articles *"Multiprocessors Computational Structures"*, N6, Taganrog (USSR), 1984, p.45-47.

6. C. Mazenc, X. Merrheim, J.-M. Muller. Computations Functions $\cos^{-1}$ and $\sin^{-1}$ Using CORDIC. *IEEE Trans. On Comp.*Vol.42, 1993, p.118-122.

7. S.-F. Hsiao, J.-M. Delosme, "Householder CORDIC algorithms", *IEEE Trans. on Computers,* vol. 44, pp. 900-1002, 1995.

8. J.P. Ward, *Quaternions and Cayley Numbers*, Kluwer Academic Publishers, 1997.

9. E. Doukhnitch, "Octonion CORDIC algorithms for DSP", in *Proc. 6th Symp. on DSP for Communication Systems, DSPCS'2002*, Sydney, Australia, Jan. 2002, pp. 159-163.

10. E. Doukhnitch, E. Ozen, "Hardware-oriented Algorithm for Quaternion Valued Matrix Decomposition", *IEEE Transactions on Circuits and Systems--II: Express Briefs*, vol. 58, no. 4, pp.225-229, 2011

11. E.I. Doukhnitch. Hardware-oriented algorithms for fast Householder transform, In Proc.Intern.Conf. on Intelligent Multiprocessor Systems, Taganrog, Russia, 1999, p. 44-48

12. Yang, B., and Böhme, J. F.: 'Reducing the computations of the singular value decomposition array given by Brent and Luk', *SIAM J. Matrix Anal. Appl.*, 12(4):713–725, 1991.

13. James M. Ortega. Introduction to Parallel and Vector Solution of Linear Systems, Plenum Press, N. Y., 1988.

14. H.V. Henderson and S.R. Searle. "The Vec-permutation Matrix, the Vec Operator and Kronecker Products, a Review", *Linear and Multilinear Algebra*, No. 9, pp. 271-288, 1981.

15. E.I. Doukhnitch, A.V. Kalyaev, "Algorithms for implementation of tensors components transformation", *Automatic and Computing Technique*, Riga, vol.2, pp.79-82, 1977

16. E. Doukhnitch, M. Salamah, A. Andreev, "Effective Processor for Matrix Decomposition', *Arabian Journal for Science and Engineering*, September 2013, p.1-7.

17. Yu Hen Hu, "The Quantization Effects of the CORDIC Algorithm", *IEEE Transactions on Signal Processing,* Vol. 40, No. 4, pp. 834-844, 1992.

18. F.Z. Zhang, "Quaternions and matrices of quaternions", *Linear Algebra Appl.* 251, pp. 21–57, 1997.

19. N. Le Bihan and S. J. Sangwine. "Jacobi method for quaternion matrix singular value decomposition", *Applied Mathematics and Computation,* 187, pp. 1265-1271, 2007.

20. E. Doukhnitch, V. Podbelskiy, "Higher Parallel Hardware-oriented Algorithm for Jacobi SVD of Quaternion Valued Matrix", *Parallel and Cloud Computing Research*, vol. 1, no.3, pp.41-49, October 2013

21. S. Paul, J. Gotze, M. Sauer, "Error Analisys of CORDIC-Based Jacobi Algorithms", *IEEE Trans. on Computers*, vol. 44, no. 7, pp. 947-951, 1995.

22. T. Nagase, M. Komata, T. Araki, " Secure signals transmission based on quaternion encryption scheme", in Proc. 18th Int. Conf., Advanced Information Networking and Application (AINA' 04), IEEE Computer Society, pp. 35-38, 2004.

23. T. Nagase, R. Koide, T. Araki, Y. Hasegawa, "A new quadripartite public-key cryptosystem," International Symposium on Communications and Information Technologies 2004 (ISCIT 2004), Sapporo, Japan, pp. 74-79, Oct. 2004.

24. T. Nagase, R. Koide, T. Araki, Y. Hasegawa, "Dispersion of sequences for generating a robust enciphering system," *ECTI Trans. Computer and Information Theory*, vol. 1, no. 1, pp. 9-14, May 2005.

25. Ehsan Malekian, Ali Zakerolhosseini, " NTRU-Like Public Key Cryptosystems beyond Dedekind Domain up to Alternative Algebra", *Transactions on Computational Science*, no. 10, pp. 25-41, 2010.

26. E. Malekian, A. Zakerolhosseini, "OTRU: A non-associative and high speed public key cryptosystem", In Proc. of the 15th CSI International Symposium "Computer Architecture and Digital Systems (CADS)", pp. 83-90, 2010

27. W. Stallings, Cryptography and Network Security, Prentice Hall, Upper Saddle River, pp. 41-46, 2006

28. S.-F.Hsiao, J.-M. Delosme "Parallel Processing of Complex Data Using Quaternion and Pseudo-Quaternion CORDIC Algorithms." In Proceedings of the ASAP'94 Conf., University of California, pp.125-130, 1994.

29. E. Doukhnitch, A. Chefranov, A. Mahmoud, "Encryption Schemes with Hyper-Complex Number Systems and their Hardware-Oriented Implementation". In the book: Theory and Practice of Cryptography Solutions for Secure Information Systems, pp. 110-133, Publisher: IGI Global, USA, 2013.

30. Hossam E.H, Ahmed H.M, Osama S.F. " An Efficient Chaos-Based Feedback Stream Cipher (ECBFSC) for Image Encryption and Decryption," Journal of Computing and Informatics, pp. 121-129, 2007

31. S.J. Sangwine, "Fourier transforms of color images using quaternions, or hypercomplex, numbers," *Electronics letters*, vol. 32, no. 21, pp. 1979-1980, 1996.

32. E. Doukhnitch, M. Salamah, "General Approach to Simple Algorithms for 2-D Positioning Techniques in Cellular Networks", *"Computer Communications"*, Volume 31, Issue 10, pp. 2185-2194, June 2008.

33. E. Doukhnitch, E. Ozen, M. Salamah, "An Efficient Approach for Trilateration in 3-D Positioning," *"Computer Communications"*, Volume 31, Issue 17, pp. 4124-4129, Nov. 2008.

www.ingramcontent.com/pod-product-compliance
Lightning Source LLC
Chambersburg PA
CBHW051209050326
40689CB00008B/1253